How **love**actually **ruined Christmas**

How **love**actually **ruined Christmas**

(or Colourful Narcotics)

Gary **Raymond**

PARTHIAN

Parthian Books
The Old Surgery
Napier Street
Cardigan
SA43 1ED

www.parthianbooks.co.uk

© Gary Raymond 2020
First published 2020
All Rights Reserved

ISBN 978-1-913640-21-7
eISBN 978-1-913640-22-4

Edited by David Cottis
Cover design by Syncopated Pandemonium
Typeset by Syncopated Pandemonium
Printed and bound by 4edge Ltd

The publisher acknowledges the financial support of the
Welsh Books Council.

British Library Cataloguing in Publication Data
A cataloguing record for this book is available from the
British Library.

This book is sold subject to the condition that it shall not by way
of trade or otherwise be circulated without the publisher's prior
consent in any form of binding or cover other than that in which
it is published.

Contents

Foreword	ix
Introduction	xiii
A Scene-by-Scene Response to *Love Actually*	1
5 Weeks to Christmas	7
4 Weeks to Christmas	47
3 Weeks to Christmas	65
2 Weeks to Christmas	79
1 Week to Christmas	111
Christmas Eve	127
1 Month Later (Epilogue)	169
Afterword	175
Acknowledgements	181
About the authors	182

*Dedicated
to all those
who have had the shit kicked out of them by*
Love Actually

Foreword

By Lisa Smithstead

I remember quite clearly the first time I saw *Love Actually*, because some trauma is hard to repress. I was an undergraduate film student at the time. As such, I was possessed of obnoxiously strong opinions about Good Film and was perhaps not the ideal target audience. As the lights went down at the university cinema, I distinctly recall a growing feeling of realisation that everyone else around me was having a very different experience. When the credits finally rolled and I turned to see friends with happy tears in their eyes declaring it to be "so lovely", I wondered if I'd somehow drifted into a parallel universe. Had everyone else been watching a different movie?

Several drinks and perplexing exchanges later ("...but it's just so *sad*", "...but it's just so *charming*", "...but wow, what a cast!"), I was willing to concede that perhaps there was in fact something wrong with *me*.

Thanks to the existence of this book, twenty-year old me finally feels validated.

If Christmas is – according to Worst Best Friend Ever Andrew Lincoln – a time when we "tell the truth", *How Love Actually Ruined Christmas* follows through on this premise with aplomb. Gary Raymond's analysis is the anti-love letter to all things Richard Curtis: a scene-by-scene take down of every paper-thin plot point, every excruciating piece of dialogue and every half-arsed characterisation.

Drawing on his considerable expertise as a critic, author and film fanatic, Raymond pulls apart what's actually wrong with *Love Actually* – from plot holes to production design and the pernicious ideology underpinning much of its lazy narrative. Raymond offers new insight into the fundamentals that the film gets wrong (what the hell is going on with the timelines in each character segment? Why exactly *is* it funny for everyone to loudly proclaim that Martine McCutcheon's character is, like, *really* fat – ha ha ha?). He also presents a fresh analysis of those scenes we think we know inside out (Alan Rickman's character, for example, might not be quite as much of a bastard as we first thought...).

When I was asked to write this foreword, I was apprehensive. Largely because it involved having to rewatch the movie. I've resisted doing so for years. Instead, I've taken miserly joy as a film studies lecturer in handing out copies of Lindy West's wonderful *Jezebel* article "I Rewatched *Love Actually* and Am Here to Ruin It for You" to crestfallen undergraduates in the final week of winter term.

As a feminist film historian and as a human woman, *Love Actually* has always bothered me. Because it's a movie in which – as many commentators have since pointed out – women are essentially voiceless. They lack any genuine agency, set up as the prizes and possessions of a network of deeply unlikeable male characters. The film follows this premise to its ultimate end by positing its most "romantic" storyline as the one in which the object of male affection is rendered wholly mute by a language barrier. Grotesquely sexist behaviour is never called out by any of the female characters, who instead cue the audience to laugh at each joke made at their expense. Add to that its overwhelming whiteness and wealth and there's a not a great deal left to like, even if Hugh Grant does do a silly dance.

When I finally settled down to rewatch it with my newborn son (apologising as I did so for inflicting this experience upon him), my initial reaction was horror at the realisation this film is over two hours long. This horror then mutated in interesting ways as the layers of Problematic that I'd never fully clocked the first-time round snowballed with the introduction of each new character. What stands out more than anything peering back into the murky waters of the early 2000s is its relentless misogyny. This turns out to be inseparable from its fatphobia, occasional casual transphobia, and cringe-inducing notion that to be British is to use "piss", "shit" and "fuck" to punctuate one's sentences – and my *gosh* isn't that all just *charming*.

I'm also guilty, though, of resisting a total dismissal of the film's merits by appealing to that one redeeming feature. That familiar plea of "I accept it's not a good film, but I *do* love the bit when..." My father-in-law, on a behind-the-scenes visit to Number 10 a few years ago, gleefully did *that* dance down *those* stairs. That's a lot of people's "moment". For others it's the flash cards. Other still have a soft spot for the precocious kid, who Raymond rightly pegs as a potential future incel. My own personal push back is "...but Emma Thompson". You know, just generally: *Emma Thompson*. It can't be *that bad* if it has Emma Thompson in it, even if it amounts to about ten minutes' total screen time. This take has been swiftly remedied, however, by reading Raymond's clear explanation here of why her character is possibly the original Karen in a film that clearly hates women.

The more I watched it, the more my love–hate obsessions with it grew, and the more this book seemed a necessary intervention to tackle that broad consensus that *Love Actually* is not just good, but a "classic" of the romcom genre. *How Love Actually Ruined Christmas* isn't simply an exercise in trashing something everyone loves, however. It's far too easy to take the contrary stance, to be That Guy for the sake of it. For all its wit, Raymond's take down is at heart a sincere intervention, highlighting the insidious aspects of the film. His analysis pinpoints a nastiness inherent within the bulk of its characterisations, and a humour fuelled by classist and sexist stereotypes that register significantly differently with hindsight.

If interrogating all that doesn't sound entirely appealing, fear not. Raymond's scene-by-scene deconstruction pulls apart the worst the film has to offer with considerable humour, always witty in its clapbacks to each offensive notion the film presents as humorously endearing. If you are equally perplexed by the popularity of this film – if you just can't understand how this random assemblage of unappealing, barely fleshed out characters even constitutes a movie – then this book is for you. If, on the other hand, you have a soft spot for it, at the very least enjoy a fresh take on things. See if we can't persuade you that, actually, as Raymond suggests, "cynicism has its uses".

Introduction

I remember reading somewhere once that the great thing about Christmas is that it's obligatory. And I suppose the best way to enjoy it is to go all in. As a child, I loved Christmas. Ranking high in the family stories trotted out every year is the one about how I used to tremble with excitement on Christmas morning as I waited to open my presents (the telling has become something of a family tradition in and of itself). A kid subsumed by the capitalist blob?[1] Sure. But back then, the deal was less with the devil, and more with the Argos catalogue.[2] Christmas Eve was time spent in the organised chaos of the extended family, involving an extensive triangle sandwich and cold meat buffet and the exchanging of the B-grade gifts between siblings, nephews, nieces, and maybe the occasional cousin. Our neighbour would dress as Father Christmas and bring his whiskey-rouged cheeks door to door along the terraces, his nicotine-stained fingers grasping a sack of plastic pickup

---

[1] As in the implacable extraterrestrial gloop that so effectively destroyed American towns in various versions of the sci-fi horror movie.
[2] The catalogue that comedian Bill Bailey once memorably to as "the laminated book of dreams".

trucks and long-legged dolls. The A-grade prezzies is what made me tremble the next morning – the stuff from the *real* Santa, i.e. my parents. I wouldn't sleep that night, of course, as the trembles set in. The longest nights of my life. There were the toys, the gluttonous excess of foods, abundance of hugs, family, the movies circled off in the *Radio Times*, everyone gathering round to watch *The Snowman* or *The Empire Strikes Back* or *Raiders of the Lost Ark* on one of the four channels. The concerted efforts to squeeze every drop of worth out of every second of the day.[3] Next year was just so far away, after all. As I grew older, I became saddened that Christmas meant less. In my twenties, there was even a brief period where I affected the cynicism of the Grinch. Perhaps, for a while, I saw that as a badge of adulthood, rolling my eyes whenever anyone looked suspiciously yule-y in the pub. I was part of a club. The Bollocks to Christmas Club. We were above it all. Cynics of the most noble stripe. But that only lasted a few years, and I came back to my rightful place as a Lover of Christmas. I crossed the floor and then crossed back again. If Christmas is obligatory, then fighting against its obligations proved a miserable bit of theatre.

Of course, it's not what it was. But nothing ever is. I grew up in the eighties, a decade that had enough problems of its own, but one that seemed to do Christmas just the way I liked it. Toys were precious, and you knew Mum and Dad had to work hard and save hard to buy them, but they weren't unobtainable, they weren't driving anybody into debt, and they weren't encouraging mass brawls in the supermarkets. Christmas was special because it didn't start in October but waited respectfully until the schools broke up before the sound of carols or Phil Spector echoed

---

[3] For more in-depth analysis about why Christmas was better in the eighties, check out the Futureheads song, "Christmas Was Better in the 80s".

in shops or the sparkle of street decorations lined the main drag through town. And the bedrock of that Christmas, the joy that we all marched to, was the folklore brought to us by Hollywood and Dickens. Stove pipe hats had been replaced by bobble hats, but apart from that nothing had changed since the chocolate tin visions of skating on frozen ponds. Bobble hats and Transformers.[4] Yes, Transformers made a difference too. All of this may be romanticised nonsense, twisted and contorted into the saccharine shapes my grown-up sensitivity needs in order to look back and cherish, but none of that matters, because Christmas is about putting a soft focus on the past and creating a fireplace in front of which we can curl up and reminisce. Your memories of childhood Christmas don't need to be historically accurate. They just serve to inform the tapestry of the good things about growing up.

It is true that Christmas changed when consumerism changed. I'm sure there was a lot of shit around when I was a kid, but I was insulated from it by a blanket woven from the sacred spools of ignorance, naivety, and freedom from the rulebook of what constituted shit and what constituted valuable artefacts. That's why I loved the VHS copy of *Howard the Duck* my dad regularly rented for me at my request from the local video shop as much as I loved the *Holst's Planet Suite* LP that my grandfather used to play to me. So, I have no inclination to look down on the fan of shit. I'm a fan of shit myself. I like nothing more than to sit down with a bag of chewy sweets and watch an eighties slasher movie. In recent years, I have become fascinated with the right-wing Christmas movie phenomenon as best exemplified by Hallmark, branching out from

---

[4] A very popular toy in the 1980s, the golden age of toys; Transformers has since been besmirched by the brash and prurient Michael Bay movie franchise. In the eighties, Transformers was just brash.

greeting cards to home cinema to fill our Christmases with actors from forgotten nineties television programmes saving their hometown of WASPville, Connecticut, in time for the Christmas Ball. I like television cooking competitions, but not the British ones that are characterised by the gumption of the competitors and the wit of the presenters; no, I like the Australian shows, the ones that come out of the screen at you as if you are being beaten to death by a thousand ashcan lids during Mardi Gras. What I'm saying is, I'm no snob. I believe in the visceral manipulative power of the screen, what Ingmar Bergman once said was the ability for film to go "directly to our feelings, deep down into the dark rooms of the soul".[5] And since his day, the most popular (as in the stuff watched by the broadest audience figures) filmmakers more and more are bypassing script-craft and character depth for sledgehammer signposting. Why infer what a character is feeling, when you can douse the whole scene with a petrochemical soundtrack? This kind of filmmaking can bring you joy without any depth of entanglement. It can make you weep for people whose names, in the midst of the blubbing, you would not be able to recall if a gun was put to your head. This shit washes over you, and it may not smell of roses, but it doesn't necessarily leave you with some terrible disease.[6] But low-demand trash must have some rules, some structure, must be made by people who know exactly what it is they are serving up.[7] You enter into a contract with these artists, one that promises thrills

---

[5] Granted, he was probably thinking of *Cries and Whispers* rather than *My Kitchen Rules: Australia*, but I think his point applies here too.

[6] Arguments to the contrary are acknowledged. I am available to argue either side of the degradation of culture debate for a reasonable fee.

[7] A perfect and popular purveyor of such joyous rubbish today would be actors like Jason Statham or Gerard Butler.

and titillation, in return for which we viewers will forgive, and even indulge, a great deal. What is unacceptable is a work that is boring, or worse; a work that thinks it's something that it isn't.

*

I guess if there was a tribe to which I was never going to admit to belonging as a youngster it was the Guild of Appreciators of Romantic Comedies.[8] And not simply the screwball comedies of Golden Era Hollywood, such as *My Man Godfrey* (1936) or *The Philadelphia Story* (1940), which brought a certain cachet by the time I was mid-teens because "old movies" had a literary cool about them. I could also get away with banging on about *Roman Holiday* (1953) and *Breakfast at Tiffany's* (1961) for hours on end because Audrey Hepburn was an icon. But you wouldn't really get away with calling these films "romantic comedies", even though that's what they are. The romcom, to me and my friends in the nineties, was defined by films like *When Harry Met Sally* (1989), which we admired because Billy Crystal was a smartass just like we wanted to be, eating fries and offering quips on life and writing about sport for a living. It wasn't because it was a beautifully structured and funny romantic story. Harry was a child; that's why we responded to that film. What you definitely couldn't get away with was losing yourself in *Sleepless in Seattle* (1993) or *You've Got Mail* (1999), and you wouldn't find any of us sitting around at parties picking apart *Four Weddings and a Funeral* (1994), even though we'd all seen these films, and we'd all liked[9] them. Nowadays, of course, we're all grown-ups, and we can

---

[8] Not a real guild.
[9] For "liked" you might also read "were moved by", "cried to", or even "enjoyed".

all have grown-up conversations about how great these movies are, and we can even stay up past our bedtime because some deep-dive channel hopping has brought us face to face with *Roxanne* (1987) or *Working Girl* (1988). The politics of these films are often questionable, and sometimes the character motivation calls for some forgiveness too. That's to the credit of the writers and directors, like Kevin Wade and Mike Nichols who get us to side with Melanie Griffiths over Sigourney Weaver in *Working Girl*, when a slight shift in perspective would probably upend that boat trip without much fuss.[10] We let a lot slide, because we're in this for something else, for that shower, not of shit, really, but of something elating, something that tells us love is a power stronger than cynicism. And *cynicism*, as a modern concept driven by the snakes of capitalism,[11] the one that makes everything feel cheap and nasty, is where creativity, and sentimental manifestations of it, meets Christmas. By which I mean the modern version of Christmas, the Michael Bay version, not the eighties Transformers version.

Hallmark movies are one thing, but the film towards which we are slowly gliding, and the subject of this book, is something else. With Hallmark movies, nobody is professing to have taken these Republican Party seasonal flat-pack turds to heart. Those of us drawn to them are drawn to them because of both an intellectual fascination with awfulness, but also an unashamed welcoming of trash into our lives. The politics of movies such as *Christmas on Honeysuckle Lane* (2018) and *The Mistletoe Promise* (2016) are clear and unambiguous: Jesus was a white man who

---

[10] That Sigourney Weaver's character in this film, who, it can be easily argued, is just Melanie Griffiths in fifteen years' time, is cast as the villain, is quite a trick.

[11] Rather than the Ancient Greek school of philosophy founded by Antisthenes, which espouses, among other things, the corrupting power of pleasure.

undoubtedly voted for Ronald Reagan. But they are predominantly conservative, family values movies, and the rather more unpalatable connotations of American centre-right politics are on the periphery if not entirely absent altogether. Nobody is encouraging children to take drugs, very rarely are we asked to side with a sexual predator, and the scripts are notably scarce of misogynistic jokes, or transphobic jokes, or homophobic jokes, or ableist jokes, or indeed any jokes that sneer and snark. I understand why people like Hallmark movies at Christmas. That's why I haven't written a book about them. There is no allure of the quest in writing that book. What I have become interested in, and something I have bored a litany of friends with over the years, is why, oh why could anybody possibly like *Love Actually*?

*

The Love for *Love Actually* is real. It is out there and it's a powerful thing. A non-scientific survey[12] conducted during the writing of this book brought an interesting array of responses to the question: What do you think of *Love Actually*? There was no indifference. One friend said they hated the trailer so much they didn't need to see the movie and have their rage codified in the compartments of scenes that make up the movie. Of those who had seen it, I hesitate to say the responses were split between those who analysed the film, and despised it, and those who simply expressed an emotional reaction to it. Haters cited overwhelmingly the misogyny of the film. They also broke down the narrative strands that make no sense, the characters they wanted to set fire to, the unearned schmaltz,[13] the class politics, the

---

[12] Predominantly made up of people I talk to via WhatsApp.
[13] Rather than try and define schmaltz here, may I be permitted to direct the reader to Carl Wilson's unsurpassed essay on the origins of schmaltz in his brilliant book *Let's Talk About Love:*

lazy and offensive comedy, the paper-thin characterisation, the offensive representation of mental illness, of sexual politics, and of women in general. Indeed, more than a few of the respondents to my question could have written their own version of this book. Lovers of *Love Actually*, however, tended to be more direct, less circumspect. They just love love love it. It was referred to as a "favourite Christmas movie ever", "love that film", "don't spoil it for me", and it was variously described as "hilarious" "heart-warming" and, wait for it, "the perfect Christmas film". I like to think that none of my friends are particularly problematic in their views and politics. I wouldn't like to assume anything, but my knowledge of these friends suggests to me that if they knew anybody in person who behaved the way most of the characters behave in *Love Actually*, they would definitely be pulled up on it. Yet, within the frame of that screen, on this occasion, and during the decades of social progress we have made since the film hit cinemas in 2003, critical faculties appear to have been put on hold. Why is that? What is the power of *Love Actually* to do this to people I love? I hope I have explained that I understand, and, on the whole, am an advocate for, the existence and enjoyment of shit. As one MGM scriptwriter was fond of saying in the 1940s, "shit has its own integrity".[14] But I never saw any integrity in *Love Actually*. What did I miss? I have only ever seen a tone-deaf, offensive, badly made movie with an execrable script and dire performances, all cast to a backdrop of ugly cynicism and a dubious moral compass. But this has never been enough to turn some people away. Indeed, not just turn

---

Why Other People Have Such Bad Taste (Bloomsbury, 2007) in the chapter "Let's Talk About Schmaltz".
[14] Gore Vidal starts his annual retrospective for *The New York Review of Books* on the bestselling books of 1972 by quoting the line of an anonymous Hollywood writer friend who he only ever refers to as The Wise Hack.

them away. *Love Actually* boasted a £250 million box office (off the back of £40m budget). People love love love *Love Actually*. But to love it, one must suspend all critical faculties, surely? Toss to the wind any sensitivities about entire groups of society that society would do better to be sensitive about? Or have I misunderstood something about it? Have I been overthinking it? Or underthinking it? Or thinking about it in the wrong way? Perhaps now, with a pen and notebook in hand, I am better equipped to understand its allure. Now that I have ten years as a critic under my belt, and undoubtedly a more compassionate approach to other people's baffling admirations than I admittedly might have had when the film came out and I was twenty-four, I think I can give *Love Actually* something better than the benefit of the doubt: I'm going to give it my undivided attention.

*

Preparing to write a book like this, where you are ready – nay, hopeful – of having existing views counterbalanced or even upturned – can be a precarious business. Reading up on *Love Actually* has rarely offered me any hope.

I recently read a typical paragraph that said, "*Love Actually* oddly has a tendency to be underrated, dismissed as too cutesy or misogynistic... And all of that, in fairness, is true. But it's also a real classic of the form – masterfully structured, endlessly watchable."[15] This passage was written in 2020, in *The Independent*, a publication known for much of its hard-copy life as a serious British newspaper where you could go for serious thoughtful journalism.[16] The arti-

---

[15] This was written in the entry for *Love Actually*, 13th in a "34 best romantic comedies ever" list for UK newspaper *The Independent* in 2020.

[16] A reputation laid waste during newspaper journalism's scorched-earth defeat at the hands of the internet.

cle admits *Love Actually* is misogynistic, but then dismisses what can only be best described as the *concerns* of people who point out the misogyny, and goes on to say that *Love Actually* is "masterfully structured" (it's *not*; it's a mess, and even writer–director Richard Curtis has spoken of the "nightmare" of the editing process). It is referred to as a "classic of the form" (a common defence), yet we are not too sure what "form" here is being referenced. Christmas movie? Romantic comedy? Compare *Love Actually* like for like, to save confusion, with Richard Curtis's other high-achieving forays into romcom (as writer and/or director), such as *Four Weddings and a Funeral* (1994), *Notting Hill* (1999), or *Bridget Jones's Diary* (2001). All of these films are what we can politely now tag "dated", but they stand up remarkably well as comedies, full of snappy dialogue, good performances, and winning romantic narrative arcs. They have the air of authenticity about them, with a healthy mix of stock comedic types and well-drawn central characters. Renée Zellweger's Bridget Jones may not quite be the everywoman of the class of 2020, but was certainly, and thankfully, recognised by millions of women in 2001 as someone they could relate to. *Four Weddings…* has the charm of English eccentricities pitted against the pragmatism of American glamour. *Notting Hill* repeats that riff, but with similarly charming effect. I don't remember *Love Actually* reaching any of those arguably modest creative heights. And what's worse, *Love Actually* has nothing to do with Christmas. It just attaches itself to Christmas like a parasite and feeds off its sentimentality whilst pumping the host full of schmaltz. I think of *Love Actually* as a lazy, tired, and ironically frenetic shambles. That the three movies mentioned above are the three that directly preceded *Love Actually* might account for some of the imagination fatigue on display. It cannot be the twisted creation of a sick mind. Richard Curtis is not a right-wing degenerate figure. A reasonable defence of him here could be that he overreached and did it at a time when he was creatively exhausted. So, I'm not setting myself up to accuse anyone of anything. I just want to know why – *how!* – people love *Love Actually* so much?

*

Reading reviews of *Love Actually*, I one day read Michael Atkinson's piece for *The Village Voice*. In his generally middling reaction to the film, Atkinson wrote that the film was populated with "colourful neurotics".[17] But I misread this. I read "colourful narcotics". I carried this judgment around with me for years, thinking it a brilliant summation of the allure of the movie, summing up its baffling popularity, the hold it has over people, making them unable to see its glaring flaws, its offensive attitudes, its chauvinism, its misogyny, its cruelness and superficiality, its one-dimensional characters, its nonsensical storylines, its creepy stalkers, its irredeemably terrible men, its weak and weeping women, its confusing timelines, its hanging narrative threads, its imbalance, its bad jokes, its schmaltz, the terrible music selected for its terrible soundtrack, its leery obsession with supermodels, its attitude to children, to the working class, to mental health, its politics of privilege, its Chipping Norton Toryism... (I could go on, but let's save something for the main commentary). The "colourful narcotics" is a drug that dulls the critical senses, that clouds people's judgement, making those susceptible to its hallucinogenic powers think they've seen a funny, warm-hearted, romantic film about the many complex manifestations of love. "Colourful narcotics". A perfect description.

When I realised that Atkinson had not written that

---

[17] A review in *The Village Voice* from November 2003 on the release of the movie in the US.

perfect two-word review, and that he had in fact somehow identified "colourful neurotics" in the parade of dull characters *Love Actually* bombards us with, I felt not just confused but slightly betrayed. Betrayed by a critic who had no idea he had been serving me so well for so many years. I had agreed with a point he had artfully not made. It then became the title for a book I always assumed I would never write. "Colourful Narcotics" explains to the initiated what I would hope to uncover in a fresh scene-by-scene analysis of the film; it would act as a metaphor for the effect I was sure to encounter with my critical faculties positioned in the appropriate "critical receive position". It would also serve my ego, giving a book about a romantic comedy a bit of literary heft. The lockdown in reaction to the 2020 global pandemic meant that I had an opportunity to write the book I had only ever imagined was a joke I would trot out down the pub or at dinner, a feebly constructed framework from which I could launch another attack on the film to like-minded people. *One day! One day, I will write a book about that film!* So, I did it. This is my lockdown book, in much the same way *Love Actually* is Richard Curtis's 9/11 movie.[18] The idea of the "colourful narcotic" was the one that sent me into the viewing, and from which the scene-by-scene commentary that follows – the full package: the title, the concept, and now the actual text. By the time it came back from my publisher, the most glaring note was that the title is going to have to be *How Love Actually Ruined Christmas*. Cynicism has it uses, and Christmas will never be like it was in the eighties, whether *Love Actually* has anything to do with it or not.

---

[18] Which is to say it has nothing to do with the pandemic, but I'll probably talk about how it was inspired by it.

A ~~Scene-by-Scene~~ Response to **love**actually

Prologue

We begin by landing on the moon – or is it *Music for Airports*?[19] – soft, warm, ambient chords rise out of synthesisers, rise out of nowhere, and we can focus, and it's not the surface of the moon, like when Brian Eno soundtracked the Apollo landings, but it is an airport. The first few seconds shiver us awake. The chords are transporting us, the curtain is rising on this festive delight; families are uniting, there are broad smiles, tears of joy, a little girl with braces, an old woman thankful for every second she has left. We won't be going too much for subtlety here. Writer–director Richard Curtis has sent his camera crew out to hang around in the arrivals lounge of Heathrow and secretly film people embracing as they return from abroad/welcome back returnees. The crew did ask permission of the ones who made the cut. A mischievous part of me is disappointed by this diligence. It takes the edge off the experience of watching them. The idea of people sitting in the cinema a year

---

[19] *Ambient 1: Music for Airports* (Polydor, 1978) was the first of four "ambient" albums by Brian Eno. Eno is widely regarded as having invented ambient music with this record, and the reach of its influence cannot be overestimated. It even reaches to *Love Actually*, after all.

later rubbing their eyes and exclaiming, *Is that Me?!?* But it matters, I suppose, that this is real footage, filmed with the tacky jiggedy verité of noughties camcorder standard definition. This is real. Real airport joy.

A voice-over. We can recognise Hugh Grant's dulcet tones, locked in with his unmoving lower jaw, and probably would have been able to do so even easier in 2003 when he was one of the biggest film stars in the world. His brand – foppish, bumbling, toff charm – was unique at the time. He had cornered the market better than any English actor to have gone before. It was only a matter of time before somebody made him Prime Minister.[20] This is a prologue, but rather than a minor character, a Herald, or Servant, pushed out from behind the curtain to lay out the story we are about watch unfold, this is the Prime Minister of Great Britain and Northern Ireland. His speech, less Churchillian and more Christmas card.

Curtis the writer, in no uncertain terms, is here attempting the classic literary opening. What you are about to watch is a simple tale, he says, but one that will reach deep into the most profound of human experiences. It is like Tolstoy getting to the heart of the family,[21] or Graham Greene getting to his crumbling Catholicism.[22] Curtis is letting us know that *Love Actually* is going to be a crushingly sentimental journey through the nature of human love by way of complex geopolitics. Yes: PM Hugh Grant, in his prologue speech, mentions 9/11. It's probably important, tonally,

---

[20] It could be argued that in the UK nowadays Grant is just as well known for his anti-establishment activism, and therefore his opportunity to grab the job has probably passed him by.

[21] The opening line of Tolstoy's *Anna Karenina* (1873–77) is generally regarded as the greatest in all literature.

[22] The opening passage of Grahame Greene's *The End of the Affair* (1951) is regarded by Zadie Smith as the best opening of a novel, and that's good enough for me.

to remember that the Twin Towers went down almost exactly two years before *Love Actually* hit cinema screens. You could convincingly argue that *Love Actually* is Curtis's response to 9/11. As we go on, we will come to understand just what a screwed-up, dark, and misjudged reaction that was.

Fade to black.

5 Weeks to Christmas

When we fade up, we fade up to the concentrating face of Bill Nighy, one of many British national treasures who over the next two hours and ten minutes will turn their considerable skills to the efforts of encouraging me to eat my own face.

Love Actually is a film, we all know, that many people love. But those who hate it, those who feel it is perhaps one of the most significant low points in humankind's gleeful race to the bottom, often speak of the bits in it that they enjoy. Most people who hate *Love Actually* offer up one character, one scene, that they like. It goes something like this. "Yes, *Love Actually* is abhorrent, offensive, stupid, crass, lazy, but y'know, Bill Nighy is good." I am here to tell you, reader, that the case for Nighy is likely to be the most compelling evidence for the conspiracy theory (that I may have had a hand in propagating) that some national hypnosis has been in operation when it comes to this film,[23] a trick played by the devil, evidence of the effect of these colourful narcotics.

---

[23] In 2017, when being interviewed on Australian chatshow, *The Project*, Bill Nighy said that if he gets an epitaph it will be his most famous line from *Love Actually*, "Kids, don't buy drugs… become a rock star and people will give you them for free."

Nighy is here to enact part two of the opening salvo of *Love Actually*, after PM Hugh Grant has told us what to expect, that this is going to be uplifting, that it will be about all the forms of love that there is in this hill of beans of a world, and that the world is a good place peopled with good peoples, and even as the Twin Towers came down all that could be heard for miles around was not the screams of thousands mixed with the hellish crunch of twisting metal, but was the ethereal, Eno-laced sentiment that Love, actually, is all around. Yes, here comes Nighy singing your Christmas Number One for 2003, a smooth candy pop cover version of Wet Wet Wet doing a smooth glitzy cover version of the Troggs song that isn't "Wild Thing". Nighy seems to be channelling Keith Richards just a little, in so much as he's very old, drug-battered, and cannot sing a note. But his Billy Mack – who sounds more like a Viz character who goes around wanking into other people's Happy Meals than an aging national treasure rock star – is only slightly an homage to Johnny Depp gurning his way through fifty-seven *Pirates of the Caribbean* movies as Keith Richards. You have to admit there is more to Mack than Jack Sparrow. And more of the devil in him too.

Billy records from a seated position on a stool. This may explain why his vocal is so short on breath. But he has *some* energy, as he shows when he does a little dance, swinging his arms and pouting like an old street drunk who's just been woken up by a road sweeper, only the top half of him apparently being able to really get into the groove.

The track is cut short. Billy has got the words wrong. This is a novelty record, and the lyrics have been rewritten to cast a wink at the Christmas market. This is to be a *reimagining*. Rab C. Nesbitt[24] is in the production booth,

---

[24] Actor Gregor Fisher will forever only be Rab C. Nesbitt to at least one generation.

scrubbed up from his string vest into a fetching double denim. He already looks frustrated, tired, his mind half on going back to the concrete benches round the back of Woolworths with a plastic bag full of McEwan's Extra. Billy is a maverick, you see; the type of maverick we are supposed to find charming, the type who is feckless and lazy and supremely entitled, the type who walks around thinking all lobbies of four-star hotels are decorated with the tufts of the torn-out hair of personal assistants. Billy may not be wanking into your quarter pounder, but he's definitely a wanker.[25]

It's difficult to describe how much this post-prologue scene makes me feel nauseous. For a start, I know what hell is to come, and there is still so far to go; but also it's the half-hearted confidence of the whole thing, the fact everybody involved in the film knows this is going to be huge and they really don't have to work too hard at it. Rab C.'s little jiggle is presumably supposed to be funny, because overweight men doing a slightly effeminate hip wiggle is funny. Bill Nighy can't be arsed to stand up from his stool.

---

[25] A word here about the way characters are drawn in *Love Actually*. It would be something if we had some idea of who Billy Mack is, where he comes from, what his achievements have been, to give him the status he holds throughout the film. Unlike old rockers like Elton John and Paul McCartney he neither seems to have a formidable back catalogue, nor is he partnering up with the Young Turks of the day, like Elton did with Blue, or McCartney did with Kanye. He is just *there*, born in the moment, a creation of the mind of a writer who perhaps doesn't know anything about the music business, and even less about rock 'n' roll. Consider the character's baffling popularity. Counterintuitively, it's also a shame that no spin-off Billy Mack movie was made, telling his life story from early childhood in the slums of Glasgow, where he first meets Rab C. Nesbitt, who will go on to turn his own life around using Billy Mack as the crutch on which to hoist himself and find a goal, a meaning, self-worth. An inspiring story, potentially, that we can perhaps see played out to semi-tragic consequences within the walls of this film.

The song they are recording, "Love Is All Around", is a decent hippy ballad, made sickeningly schmaltzy by Marty Pellow's goateed smirk for Richard Curtis's previous rom-com behemoth, *Four Weddings and a Funeral* (1994). Curtis couldn't even be bothered to find a different song. It's a regurgitation. A lazy, sleek turd of a song.[26] *And* it drives a direct line between that dreadful recording and this dreadful movie. If you ever wondered what soulless bastards buy Wet Wet Wet singles, now you know: the people who went on to make *Love Actually*.

But then something miraculous happens. Meta does what Meta wants. And there is the smallest hint that this whole film is a joke, and that the joke is on the viewer. The joke is on *us*.

All of a sudden, *I'm interested*.

Billy Mack, singing the shit lyrics adapted from the original slightly less shit lyrics looks almost straight into the camera and stops and says, "This is shit." In the control booth, Rab C. looks almost right into the camera too, and says in a thick Scottish brogue, "That's right: *solid-gold shit*." Can it be he doesn't mean only the song? Can it be he means the entire film? The only sentence of sense in the entire movie, and it comes of course, from the Glaswegian homeless drunk, as if he has gatecrashed this Notting Hill nightmare to speak truth to power.

There is hope for us yet.

---

[26] The use of this song is made all the more difficult to reconcile with given that A Girl Called Eddy (AKA Erin Moran) wrote a song called "Love Actually" for this film, a beautiful Bacharach-esque ballad that ended up as a B-side to Moran's "Somebody Hurt You" in 2004. Richard Curtis might have presented this worthy talent to the world through his film. But he chose not to for some reason or another, instead rehashing "Love Is All Around".

Montage

Some set-up next.

Atmosphere. The painting of backdrops. Various parts of London at Christmas. Probably iconic Christmas scenes of the modern metropolitan London. I don't care, and I won't be looking them up, because nothing bores me more than London referencing itself. There's an ice rink. Is it in front of St James's Palace? Is that in London? Is that even a palace? Who gives a shit, really? I recognise the London Eye – not Christmassy in itself, although we do always get to see it when the New Year's Eve fireworks go off. But really, it's London. This is a Richard Curtis movie. He's the Woody Allen of Hammersmith. Everything will be clean, dreamy. If there are money concerns, it will be because one character is an accountant on a six-figure salary who has been found skimming off the top. There won't be a wind-blown crisp packet in sight.

After the two minutes of Billy Mack mocking us to our faces, we are straight in. *Love Actually* is a compendium film, not ensemble, as very rarely do characters come together other than in slightly convoluted ways. It is a film structured through several extremely frenetic strands, each of them purportedly exploring different facets of "love",[27] although as we shall we see, these are muddy, lazy attempts at doing so, and many of the strands are left hanging like shoelace drool from a big dog's mouth.

---

[27] *Love Actually* is really only about *eros*, the Greek term for romantic sexual love, although there are moments of *storge*, or familial love, some traces of *philia*, or platonic love (although also much stronger examples of friends treating other friends very badly indeed), and, at a stretch, perhaps an example of *xenia*, the love shown when accepting a guest into your home, as seen when Colin becomes a sex tourist.

Jamie & Jamie's Girlfriend

Colin Firth looking for his keys. His girlfriend is in bed with a big red nose, complaining of a cold. Good bit of character foreshadowing here. Firth's Jamie likes younger, beautiful, vulnerable women. Soon we will discover she is having an affair. And with his brother. She could not be a worse human being. Jamie's Girlfriend, not given a name unfortunately (how hard would it have been to just pluck a Bunty, or Ginnie, or Elderflower out of the air?), is the first of many minor characters I would like to have followed out of the narrative during the course of the movie. I will call these *Escapees*. Jamie's Girlfriend is Escapee One. We are meant to view her as villain, because she cheats on Colin Firth.[28] Jamie is supposed to be charming, busy

---

[28] *Love Actually* frequently uses the star power of its actors to stand in for actual depth and development of its characters. Many of the characters in *Love Actually* would disintegrate in the breeze were they to be played by unknowns. Jamie's Girlfriend was an unknown, so why even give her a name? In fact, Sienna Guillory (why not call the character *Sienna*?) escapes from *Love Actually* to take up the role of ass kicker of the undead in the *Resident Evil* movie franchise, presumably forever exorcising the demons of appearing in *Love Actually* by bashing up the cadavers of brain-hungry hordes.

and handsome and fresh. "Have I told you I love you even when you're sick and disgusting?" he says. Put that line in the mouth of a character without a plummy English accent and it may come across differently. Anyway, she *is* disgusting, because she's about to cheat on Colin Firth.

But there's no time to think about that now. We have to move quickly here, because the story strands, and their attached characters, are going to be introduced like a smart bomb blitz, because they have to fit into the running time of the "Love Is All Around" song, which can only be looped a few times before viewers begin to involuntarily projectile vomit.

Daniel & Karen

Next up is Liam Neeson as Daniel. Another upwardly mobile man with an upwardly mobile name.[29] This first scene with Neeson (and with Emma Thompson's Karen) does several things at once. It sets up the first important character bombshell. Neeson's wife has recently died. Important to note this is played for laughs. Thompson (Karen is Daniel's best friend) is being busy with a pepper in her kitchen and doesn't really have time to talk with Daniel at the moment. Karen's daughter is trying to explain that she is to play a lobster in the school nativity. "How many lobsters were at the birth of Jesus?" says Thompson, incredulously, as her oh-so-cute daughter says things no actual child would say like *Duh*. (At this point Jordan Peterson lights a cigarette from his spotlight at the kitchen table and explains how everyone at the birth of Jesus was a lobster, and Jesus was the biggest, fiercest, most upwardly mobile lobster of them all.[30]) Thompson can't talk, though,

---

[29] There is no imagination injected into the naming of characters in *Love Actually*. It is as if Curtis sees every character as an everyman. Even the women.

[30] Professor Jordan Peterson famously used the hierarchical structures of the lobsterverse to argue his theories on gender dynamics.

even though Neeson has nobody else to talk to. He's obviously already doing everyone's head in with his banging on about his "recently dead wife". What a bore. "Love Is All Around" should reach a climax here, but it doesn't quite get off the ground.

What this scene does is tell us Daniel is lonely, and that his wife has died, but he has a pretty good sense of humour about it. It also tells us he's upwardly mobile, and that wives dying is pretty manageable for men who live in a central London mews and have lots of box files in their home office. We also learn that a second peripheral character has no name. The wife. The dead wife. Just died. The wife just died. It already begins to feel like a Hancock sketch. "The wife just died." Lifts pint to sagging mouth.

We also learn Thompson's Karen is no nonsense. Yes, your wife died but don't you think it's time to move on? Yes, *just* died, I said *just*, didn't I? It's been weeks. What are all those box files for if not printouts of prospective replacement wives? Also, to be called WIFE.

Colin

Very quick introduction to Colin, perhaps the most repulsive sex pest in a movie filled with sex pests. Actor Kris Marshall, a delightful human in real life (no doubt), has the unenviable skill of embodying characters you just want to push into oncoming traffic. As the son in long-running and bafflingly popular TV sitcom *My Family* (2000–11), he took the idea of the layabout entitled manchild to new heights – to an artform, you could even say. He is obviously hired here to provide similar charms. The problem is, in *My Family*, Marshall had several years to bed in, to have some fun, and although it's obvious no Kris Marshall character is ever going to grow up to treat women with respect, you could warm to him because his lifelong project of winding up his neurotic father, played by Robert Lindsay, was something you could get on board with. Colin doesn't have the advantage of such space. It is almost certain that, at his birth, the midwife punched Colin in the face rather than smacking his arse. It would have been instinct, almost a duty.

Possibly, Colin is the first attempt at a working-class character in *Love Actually* (although later scenes stomp all over this impression); he has a low-level job delivering sandwiches and crisps to office workers, and engaging in low-level sexual harassment of the women there. "Want to try some of my nuts?" "A beautiful muffin for a beautiful lady." "Slice of mango for my future wife?" Future Wife is Mia, who rolls her eyes at him, because he's both a creep and a harmless[31] nobody not worth the ear time. She, we will soon discover, has her sights set on more sophisticated goals.

---

[31] Colin might also be a future serial killer, chased around Hackney by DCI John Luther – I think it's the *Quadrophenia* parka coat that does it. Once you envisage Colin as an early-years serial killer, you cannot shake that destiny for him from your mind. Everything else slips into place. I do like to imagine the future lives of some of these characters popping up in other shows. As an interesting footnote to a footnote, Jamie's unnamed girlfriend is played by Sienna Guillory, who, as well as her *Resident Evil* role, sparks a relationship with DCI John Luther, or rather her character Mary Day does, when she drives into the back of his car at a junction in season three of the BBC thriller, raising the possibility that Colin and Jamie's Girlfriend could cross paths when Colin's future serial killer plagues London.

John & Judy

I've always wondered if the John and Judy porn story strand was a Notting Hill dinner party joke that Richard Curtis felt he had to crowbar in to one of his movies at some point, because John and Judy have always felt like the names from a Ladybird children's book: *John and Judy Go Camping*, *John and Judy Bake a Cake*, *John and Judy Do Anal*. Anyway, joke or no joke, it's the most painful, least funny story strand, all based upon the outmoded idea that the English are uptight about sex. The joke is the incongruity. Throughout their scenes together, Martin Freeman and Joanna Page will talk about mundane things whilst simulating various, and increasingly outrageous, sexual acts on camera, until they finally fall in love. That's the joke.

One thing I can't escape is also the idea that throughout, they are filming softcore, non-penetrative pornography. Extremely high-end, big-budget, softcore porn. Big film crews, expensive location shooting, with two adult actors – no suggestion they are stars or even notable in their profession – looking comically bored and chattering throughout. It is supposed to suggest professionalism, that they can dissociate themselves from the vulgarity of their profession, that they can still be people despite their modes of income. Would it be so bad that they enjoyed their work? That they fell in love not because of their boring conversations and things they have in common, but because they had an electrical physical connection they discovered through their work? But no, that wouldn't do, because *Love Actually* is not about sex – or rather it is, but only a teenage boy's idea of sex. If we want to be adults, then sex is for the wedding night.

Mark & Peter

The lads. We are in close up on them both, and for a moment we cannot be sure they're not up in court, probably for sexual assault, although Peter does have the shirt and tie of an investment banker who got in over his head and is taking the fall for systemic corruption at his firm.[32]

They talk about a stag do. Peter's stag do. Mark must be his best man. God, they are handsome in that boyish, tickle-a-waitress's-arse-in-the-hospitality-box-at-Twickenham kind of way. Peter is chastising Mark for hiring "Brazilian prostitutes" for his stag do. Strangely specific. Were there websites for this kind of niche ordering in 2003? Then we discover that the "Brazilian" bit is a set up for a transphobic joke. The prostitutes, you see, turned out to be all men. A very Brazilian thing. Particularly if you're a writer like Richard Curtis who just trots this shit out without a second thought. I worry Mark wasn't quite as focused when booking these prostitutes as he should have been, given his responsibility as Best Man. Any company worth the name would surely make it clear if you were about to

---

[32] He'll do a bit of time, but they'll look after him and his family when he gets out.

order transgender sex workers or not. They would surely otherwise quickly earn themselves a professional reputation extremely damaging to the brand. Or maybe it was just implicit, when Mark specifically asked for Brazilian prostitutes. But if he did, didn't he have an idea of the sort of offensive cliché he might be letting himself in for? But this is Mark. The lad. Happy go lucky. Beer tokens in his left pockets and a wallet full of blow. And that is why the lightning bolt of love is particularly striking when it strikes. He's a lad – don't know if I mentioned. What could love possibly do for him? He's all about prozzies and pranks, and, without a shadow of doubt, mountains of cocaine.

Of course, the lightning strike will come in the form of Keira Knightley, fresh from the success of *Bend it Like Beckham* (2002), with her pubescent charms, schoolgirl dimples and a waist ready made for the hula hoop (the crispy corn snack, not the Day-Glo plastic band you twirl around your waist). Knightley is Peter's betrothed. Of course, Mark falls in love with his best mucka's missus, because he's a total twat. Selfish, entitled, a Twickenham twat. Spoiled and whining, no idea that a twat he is, although he suspects it, and he is proud of it.

Chiwetel Ejiofor has never been more wasted than he is here. It's a decade before he gets his Oscar nomination for playing Solomon Northup in *12 Years a Slave* (2013), but he's an actor who has long been leading man material in good-quality British dramas. He is good at playing troubled alpha-minus males, morally strong men who find themselves in scenarios where their moral world has been shaken, such as *12 Years...* or TV's *The Shadow Line* (2011). It's a shame Curtis decides to write this strand from the point of view of Andrew Lincoln's Mark, a much less interesting actor and character. The potential here for Ejiofor to create a tormented hero, watching his new wife and old friend run off together, is one cinema will never be blessed with.

Lincoln, however, had under his belt at that time, the role of Egg in television's *This Life* (1996–97), a man who was finding it hard to grow up, and was a bit of a twat, treating his girlfriend and young lawyer housemates to various puerile outbursts and escapades. It is perhaps telling that Richard Curtis found the journey of the twat who cannot grow up, who has no respect for his best friend, and who has emotional trauma meltdowns to the soundtrack of Dido, a more interesting arc to explore than that of a man of character fighting to keep his moral compass, as Ejiofor had already done as Othello at the Bloomsbury Theatre or as Romeo at the National (although Romeo it could be argued, is also a bit of an entitled twat[33]).

So, let's get back to just how fucked up it is to book prostitutes for your best friend's stag do. Of course, these things are not drawn from fiction. They have happened. But we probably aren't supposed to admire these men, are we? It is difficult to imagine the guffaws Curtis himself must have imagined coming out of the audience as he wrote this exchange between Mark and Peter. It brings up the question, who is this movie *for*? It's one thing to have a hit Christmas movie embraced by millions around the world, but it's another to calculate it, to know the dark places from which the movie-going public will laugh and swoon.

The camera pulls back, and it turns out that this is Peter's wedding day, not his court hearing, and the secret of the Brazilian transgender sex workers Mark booked for his stag do is cemented in the masonry of their male bond. I doubt it will even come out if Mark were to have an affair

---

[33] One of the joys of researching this book has been the unexpected Google hit, such as when I circumspectly searched the term "Is Romeo a twat" and was introduced to the ever quotable Vicky Pattison of *Geordie Shore*, who once said of one reality TV tryst that it was "like Romeo and Juliet. If Romeo was a twat".

with the woman Ejiofor is just a few minutes away from marrying. In fact, I know it doesn't, because I've seen the film before. It never gets mentioned again. This horrifying character point is just for laughs, no matter how dark the connotations. It's so we know they're lads. It's actually meant... gulp... to *endear* us to Mark.

What a lucky bride it is emerging from the soft-focus fuzz of the church doorway. The camera unfuzzes to reveal Keira Knightley, her dimples doing much of the work, that smile a rictus fix of a woman of only 18 years of age at the time of filming, already no doubt perfect for a film riddled with storylines where older men sexually harass younger women in the workplace.

But she's only there for a second.[34] We must move on. There are so many other characters, plotlines, and dubious erotic entanglements to set up.

---

[34] There is one thing *Love Actually* can most certainly not be accused of, and that is overexploiting the acting talents of Keira Knightley. She is one of many huge talents who is tragically left to swing in the breeze. In fact, you could argue the only actor required to do any heavy lifting at all is Emma Thompson.

PM & Natalie

This would normally be the basis of an entire film. We're about enter Number 10 Downing Street, the official residence of the British Prime Minister. This is his first entrance through that famous door, and he does so without much messing about, no speech, not much of a photo opp. He is obviously single, childless (or at least legitimately), and probably has charmed the electorate into giving him this job, much like Hugh Grant himself has done with movie producers his entire life. Annie is there to greet him inside, she is some kind of PA or something, and offers to introduce him to the rest of his household staff. First up is an elderly white-haired gent named Terence.[35] The PM immediately says that Terence reminds him of a hated pervert uncle he used to have. Ah, the unmistakable human touch charm of the populist electioneerer. It would be a cruel thing to say to anyone (even, maybe, a pervert, if your liberalism extends that far), but to your butler on a

---

[35] Frank Moorey, who plays Terence, died on November 20th, 2003, the day before *Love Actually* premiered in Leicester Square. So, the day after his death, when his family gathered to mourn his passing, Hugh Grant was to be seen on a forty-foot screen, telling Frank he reminded him of a pervert he used to know.

27

first meeting it seems positively sociopathic. But we are not in the world of cause and consequence, or even the world of delicately imagined characters. Hugh Grant has a brand in 2003, and it is *charming*, bumbling Britishness, the kind that built the Empire and enforced civilisation onto the savage corners of the globe. He is being funny, albeit uncouth. Of course, he is also supposed to be a Blair-esque presence. That's the general consensus. That may seem reductive now, but at the time of filming, Tony Blair was yet to send troops into Iraq (he actually did so six months before the film was released in March 2003), but more importantly, he was the only young-ish, handsome-ish, charming-ish PM this country had ever had. So, yes, there is some of Blair in Grant's PM, but despite the opening voice-over speech, and Grant's young charming energy, there is nothing deeper politically at play here.[36]

Next, the PM is introduced to Pat the Housekeeper and we have an opportunity for a bit of casual misogyny. "I'll be easier to clear up after the last lot," he says. "And no scary wife." A reference to Cherie Blair? Had Richard Curtis fallen out of favour with the cool kids of Cool Britannia?[37]

The PM is then introduced to Natalie. It's her first day too, which suggests some kind of slip-up in HR. She is nervous, and we've already seen that he is. She swears. Twice. Oh, shit I just said shit. Jokes of immense sophistication. Grant beams, presumably because he is getting the same sized cheque for one tenth of the screen time. Martine

---

[36] And as we'll see, Grant's PM, unbeknownst to everyone involved, in a creative act of staggering prescience, is more Boris Johnson than Tony Blair.

[37] Some snide consensus has been that *Love Actually* is built upon a foundation of smug Blairite politics, but this doesn't hold up, as we shall see, to even the mildest scratch to the film's superficial political skin.

McCutcheon is good casting.[38] She had won the hearts of the nation as the abused wife of aggressive thumb Grant Mitchell in *Eastenders* between 1995 and 1999. She'd also had a successful run as Eliza Doolittle at the National Theatre opposite Jonathan Pryce's Henry Higgins, for which she won an Olivier Award for Best Actress in 2002. She'd done a bit of working-class swearing in that role, but arguably to greater satirical effect. Hearing her swear in *Love Actually*, in that creased vernacular of hers, is what the Notting Hill lot find only slightly less funny than the lighting of farts. Grant (Hugh, not Mitchell) has the mission over the next few hours of making the case that this rough diamond will be worth him stepping down a class or three. The heart wants what it wants, and in this case, it wants the power dynamic of a Bill Clinton blowjob.

---

[38] Richard Curtis wrote the part for her.

Mark & Juliet & Peter

The marriage ceremony is done, the wedding vows and rings exchanged. Mark turns to Peter and thanks him for no surprises, such as Brazilian transgender sex workers. But there *is* a surprise, of course, because Mark is a twat. A choir is revealed, and Lynden David Hall emerges to sing a gospelised version of the Beatles' "All You Need Is Love". Fittingly for this movie, of all the Beatles' love songs, or indeed all the love songs ever written, "All You Need Is Love", for all of its charm and winning melody, has without doubt perhaps the inanest lyrics John Lennon ever penned. Sing along now...

> *There's nothing you can do that can't be done*
> *Nothing you can sing that can't be sung*
> *Nothing you can say, but you can learn how to play the game*
> *It's easy*
> *Nothing you can make that can't be made*
> *No one you can save that can't be saved*
> *Nothing you can do, but you can learn how to be you in time*
> *It's easy*

Utter drivel. But, as Rab C. Nesbitt nearly says in the first scene to Billy Mack, *solid-gold drivel*. The suspicion raises its head once more that the movie is a joke, and the joke is on us.

There is something here as well about tone, how this film is not to be taken literally, realistically; it is about the nonsense of Christmas magic, and, you have to feel, comes from the same ignorant blasé sentiment that penned such culturally offensive records as "Do They Know It's Christmas".

The scene itself lasts longer in the memory of the sentimental, I suspect, that it does on screen. Nothing lasts long on screen in *Love Actually*. Everything moves at such a pace it's almost difficult to keep track. Which makes the excruciating *length* of the film as a whole all the more confusing. *Love Actually* is both joltingly fast and unendurably slow. It is Schrödinger's film.

Jamie

Jamie is betrayed by his own brother. Another quick scene. Jamie pops home (he's been at Peter and Juliet's wedding, and was presumably nudged out to make room for the extended brass section) to find his own brother is banging Jamie's Girlfriend (referred to here as "the lady of the house" to navigate the choppy waters of having to name her character). She calls out to the brother – get back in here and give me a good seeing to before Jamie comes home and figures out I don't have a name – that sort of thing. Facepalm.

Colin

We're over to the wedding party, the party Jamie presumably won't attend now his life has fallen apart, and sadly that means we're in the company of Colin's punchable face, as he is gliding around offering out canapés with much the same level of charm he earlier had while handing out muffins in the office. He leers at the backsides of young female guests and generally raises the question of how he was ever hired by a catering firm in the first place. His gurning, slobbering advances are spurned by the wonderful Julia Davis in a comedic exchange where set-up and punchline dance around each other with much the same level of sophistication as Colin does around women.[39] He ducks out to the tradesman's entrance where he delivers the first shock of the movie to Tony, his oppo. Apparently, Colin is looking for "true love", which is quite the revelation, because up until that point he has come across one hundred percent as a walking hormone looking for some living tissue to dry hump. Colin, it seems, is a romantic, not a sex pest, and

---

[39] Grant reveals on the DVD commentary for *Love Actually* that this dialogue exchange was recycled from a cut sequence in *Four Weddings and a Funeral*.

again we see the moral compass of *Love Actually* flicker and flit like the altimeter of a Stuka dive bomber.

Colin has had a revelation, although it's difficult to envisage an electrical current strong enough to inspire such brain action. Charming Colin has decided the reason why no women will have sex with him – or have "true love" with him – is because they are British, and British girls are stuck up. Presumably, he has been through phases of calling them lesbians, frigid, and I was only joking you're pig ugly anyway I would never even touch you. Colin's answer is to go to America. American girls will be much easier to sexually assault, he seems to think.

John & Judy

Back on set of the porn shoot, and not a moment has passed, it seems. An entire wedding has happened in another part of London, and John and Judy have yet to take their jackets off. Perhaps there is a job here for Colin Dryhump.

But wait; the director is Tony, the same Tony who was just listening to Colin out the back of the wedding reception. So, Tony wasn't a waiter, or bell boy, or chef, or guest; in fact, he's not even a peer of Colin. He is a movie director (maybe second unit), and of big-budget, albeit adult, movies. But whatever, he probably won't crop up again as he has no love story strand of his own, so it's more likely they just didn't want to hire another actor, so filled two dramatic roles with one character. Tony. Hanging out one minute, chatting shit with his waiter friend, directing a big-budget sex movie the next. His movement from one scene to the next, though, does confuse the timeline of the interlinking stories. Is the porn movie story even the same day as the wedding story?

Tony is properly directing too. As in, he is giving direction to his actors. But then, wait, it seems this might not be a pornographic movie at all. John and Judy appear to be stand-ins. Sex body doubles? John mentions he once stood in for Brad Pitt in *Seven Years in Tibet* (1997). A peculiar random movie reference, dragooned in probably for the double whammy punchline that Martin Freeman is no Brad Pitt, and that Tibet is cold.

So, this is *not* a porn movie, which means, really, to know exactly what's going on in this strand you have to have experience of how films are made. Still, regardless of all that, we know now that Tony has done very well for himself professionally. No idea why he's friends with Colin, the very definition of total loser.

Daniel

Holy shit, it's Daniel's wife's funeral. It was *THAT* recently. Emma Thompson is a right heartless cow. She couldn't take his call because she was *chopping a fucking pepper*! And it may have even been the morning of the funeral (although as we have already established, it's tricky to figure out the timelines of *Love Actually*).

Neeson delivers a eulogy with the emotional investment of a man giving a tribute to a valued colleague who is moving on to partner at a different law firm. He recounts his wife's dying wishes, focusing on the black humour common to writers who want to use the final stages of cancer as a light-hearted but simultaneously weighty motivational plot point.[40] The banter attributed to his dead wife sends

---

[40] Ricky Gervais is perhaps a prime example of a writer guilty of this. A unique comedic talent, since moving to Los Angeles, Gervais, like Steve Martin or Larry David, seems to think he needs to prove his chops as a straight actor. He does this most often by grabbing onto the nearest lazy life tragedy in order to give him an excuse to cry in a scene. Most recently, in Netflix's *After Life*, in which Gervais bases his character's cantankerousness on the fact of his dead wife's cancer. Cancer is the lazy shorthand of emotional punch and *Love Actually* is the *Citizen Kane* of lazy shorthand.

ripples of reminiscing laughter throughout the pews of mourners. One of them, for some reason, is distinguished stage actor and greatest ever Doctor Watson, Edward Hardwicke.[41] Emma Thompson is also there, presumably finding time in her busy schedule of being the worst best friend ever to pop along to Daniel's wife's burial.

Daniel's dead wife wants to sign off with "Bye Bye Baby" by the Bay City Rollers. Neeson finally does some acting, and stares into the middle distance, tears welling in the corners of his eyes as he's reminded of her taste in music and her sense of humour, glad she's dead, if he's honest with you.

So, the coffin is carried out to the booming sound of the Bay City Rollers. Bathos, pathos, the comedy of idiosyncrasy, it's difficult to pinpoint exactly what they're going for here, other than EMOTIONS. It screams in your face. EMOTIONS.

---

[41] The deleted scenes on the DVD of *Love Actually* reveal that Edward Hardwicke, no doubt somewhat relieved to be left on the cutting room floor, was playing dead Joanna's father, so Sam's grandfather and Liam Neeson's father-in-law.

Mark & Peter & Juliet

New scene and time jump, to the arse end of the wedding do.[42] Nobody seems drunk, nobody seems narky, and Mark definitely isn't coked up, so we know this is all make-believe, the one-dimensional meanderings of a mind only interested in creating solid-gold shit.

This is where we are introduced to the idea that Mark is in love with Keira Knightley's Juliet, but more importantly, it's the place where we're introduced to Laura Linney's Sarah. Linney brings a real depth to yet another shitty part, a part that is left swinging in the breeze more than most.[43]

---

[42] On the Director's Commentary available on the *Love Actually* DVD, Richard Curtis tells a story about why he hired black comedian Junior Simpson to play the wedding DJ in this scene. He explains how he saw Simpson performing stand-up, and one of his jokes was to congratulate Curtis's film *Notting Hill* for winning the Best Special Effects Oscar for removing all black faces from the place Notting Hill. Curtis decided casting Simpson in his next film would nip that in the bud.

[43] It's interesting that few of the actors involved in *Love Actually* hardly ever talk about it in terms of a crafted piece of art. In an interview with *Wired* in 2018, Keira Knightley jokes that she can't even remember who Juliet ends up with in the movie. But on *The Graham Norton Show* in 2019, Laura Linney told one of the most heart-warming stories about the making of the film. She says

Harry & Sarah

A sophisticated note of character development here, in relative terms. Laura Linney's Sarah, at Peter and Juliet's wedding, can see that Mark is infatuated with one member of the happy couple. She seems to think it's Peter, Mark's best mate, and when he denies this, it doesn't cross her mind that twat Mark might actually be lusting after his mate's wife. Flick to whatever morning is next in this jumbled temporal dramatic space, and Alan Rickman's Harry, Harry the Affable, Harry the decent but not great Boss, calls his worker Sarah into his office to ask how long she's been in love with some other guy in the office. The other guy is described as "enigmatic", which is not how you describe a person in an off-hand way but is how a writer might clumsily describe the type of men a mousy lost-to-love female character would swoon over. It's important to remember that *Love Actually* has a lot to cram into its two-hour-fourteen-minute run time, and there is no time for show don't tell. *Tell* is much quicker.

---

how both she and her co-star Rodrigo Santoro (Enigmatic Karl) had both been dumped by their partners before shooting began and were both nursing broken hearts. She says of the scene where Sarah and Karl finally kiss, "I think there is a sweetness to that scene because of that – because we were both so sad."

Sarah is a bit sad. She's hopelessly in love, in fact. She is in love with an enigma. What could be more sad than that?[44]

It's difficult to begin to describe just how strange this scene is. In the real world, Harry the Boss is being wildly inappropriate; but even in cinematic terms, the type of advice he gives Sarah on her longing for some enigmatic rutting is usually a role reserved for the kooky best friend. Mia is sitting right outside and would be the perfect choice for someone on Sarah's level, someone who doesn't represent a top-heavy power dynamic, and someone who won't prove a headache at a HR disciplinary. But no, for some reason, Curtis goes for Harry. As Sarah cringes, seemingly half-grateful for Harry the Boss bringing to her attention that everybody knows she fancies Enigmatic Karl (there is a suggestion, but nothing more, that it might be affecting her work), because sometimes all you need in life is a simple nudge from an awkward older man sitting slightly too close to you in a work environment. "Tell him you want to have lots of sex and lots of babies. It's Christmas, for god's sake," Harry the Boss says to her. Which I think is a direct quote from the New Testament.

As Sarah moves to leave the office, Enigmatic Karl passes her in the doorway, and we learn that Enigmatic Karl is not so much enigmatic as he is foreign. What Curtis really means is that Enigmatic Karl is *exotic*, and Linney, because she is wearing a knitted tanktop, is cripplingly susceptible to the superficial lure of exoticism. All You Need Is Love, Sarah. Tell him you want babies with him. There's nothing you can make that can't be made.

---

[44] There is something to be said for the realisation Richard Curtis has that he doesn't have time to waste a single line during *Love Actually*. Every line of dialogue has to be given over to moving either the story forward, or giving a simple, thudding signpost to characterisation. For a more successful, artful, random example of this, look at the way Christopher Nolan deals with the complications of keeping plot and character turning over line by line in *Inception* (2010).

Billy Mack

Very smooth cut from Sarah asking Mia if she could turn the office radio down. The radio is playing the new Billy Mack record, the one of which we were honoured to have a glimpse of the recording session at the opening of the film. We glide on the continuity waves of the song from the office to Billy Mack being interviewed on a radio station to promote said record. Consensus is building that Mack's "Christmas Is All Around" is a terrible song, an abomination, and Curtis grins sadistically at us from over his computer screen.

Mack is interviewed by Mike (played by Marcus Brigstocke, who you'd have thought would have hated this sort of thing[45]), a wide-eyed young DJ at Radio Watford (and, incidentally, a character no more deserving of a name than

---

[45] In a 2016 interview on Richard Herring's podcast *RHLSTP*, Brigstocke talks of his love for the film, although he acknowledges it isn't very good. He also talks briefly about the cast read-through and claims that the original script was beautifully nuanced and that the film was butchered in post-production when they realised it was way too long. The scene where Mark turns up with the flashcard on Juliet's doorstep, for instance, Brigstocke claims, had much more context and development in the lead-up. (Brigstocke also says that Richard Curtis spends half of every year fundraising

Jamie's Girlfriend, but he has one anyway). Here Mack is supposed to come across as affable, honest, a cheeky chappy who has seen it all and done it all. But I'm just not so sure how pretending to have shagged Britney Spears fits into that character frame. In 2003, Bill Nighy was in his early fifties (Billy later refers to himself as being in his "mid-fifties"). Britney Spears would have been twenty-two. And this seems to have been a story from Billy Mack's past, and not recent past, because this is his comeback record. How did this union come about? Of course, we're not supposed to believe Billy, we're supposed take this as a joke, and Billy isn't really expecting us to believe it; he's painting a picture of himself of the type of man who could sleep with someone like Britney Spears – at least, at the height of his fame he could. Mike the DJ laughs along, and it's difficult now not to think of Trump's "grab 'em by the pussy" *Access Hollywood* tape, as he bragged about his sexual assault prowess. Of course, Billy Mack never slept with Britney Spears, because Billy Mack is not a real person, and Britney Spears is, so we're left with just the joke, and it begins to smell a lot like a locker room in that radio booth.[46]

Pretending Billy Mack shagged Britney Spears is definitely not funny in this day and age, and even if the joke was built around one hundred percent consenting Spears, it speaks of an unattractive attitude a washed-up old white dude can have toward brilliant young megastars if they're female. Again, we are supposed to like Billy for his irreverent attitudes to the industry of celebrity. It's likeable like a

---

for Comic Relief, and so people who hate *Love Actually* shouldn't be so mean to him about it.)

[46] Bill Nighy has since admitted regret at the Britney Spears joke, although as these regrets have always been in print, it's difficult to tell whether he's being sarcastic or not, resurrecting one of the more charmless character traits of Billy Mack.

dirty old uncle is likeable, only we've already been introduced to the idea that Prime Minister Hugh Grant hated his pervert uncle Terence, so what are we supposed to believe here? Is it about power structures? Or is pretending, on live radio, that he shagged Britney Spears supposed to be pathetic? Are we supposed to feel sorry for Billy Mack, a man torn between playing up to his own infantile, misogynist persona nurtured by an infantile and misogynist music industry, and the knowledge that he is, deep down, a sad and lonely man?

Billy goes on to give a speech about how terrible his new record is, and how "kiddies" should buy "Uncle Billy's" song to ensure he has a nice Christmas. Again, we are supposed to be endeared, presumably for his honesty and not for his cynicism, which is rarely an endearing quality in anyone.

PM & Natalie

A Cabinet meeting. On the agenda is how this new PM will not be the poodle of America, "not like the last government". Curtis continues to want to make some political points about the Blair administration. We could assume that this PM, David, Hugh Grant, is the PM Richard Curtis would prefer to see in Downing Street, rather than that Blighter Blair who took us (is currently taking us, in 2003) into an illegal war in Iraq – the type of PM who has only a couple of women in his cabinet,[47] and says things like, "Who do you have to screw to get a chocolate biscuit around here?" This joke has two functions: firstly, to remind us this PM is a bit of a maverick, coming out with lines like this the way he does, in contexts like this. Secondly, it sets up the entrance of Natalie, who now appears to be a tea lady, rather than a PA. The joke plays thus: "Who do I have to screw to get a chocolate biscuit around here?" Enter Natalie. Oh, that's awkward, because I do actually want to screw her. And I actually do want a chocolate biscuit.

---

[47] Although Blair was famous for having ushered in record numbers of women MPs to Westminster (dubbed "Blair Babes" by Britain's gutter press), he had a decent but hardly impressive ratio of women to men in Cabinet positions during his years as Prime Minister.

Cut to next scene. He is in his office. Natalie brings him some chocolate biscuits. Has he now screwed her, between scenes? No, he hasn't, because there is still some sexual tension there, and everyone knows these office shags are all about the chase, and if/when he does shag her, he'll probably have her immediately moved to another department before her dress is even back from the dry cleaners.

We are supposed to be under the impression that Hugh Grant is here a liberal Labour Prime Minister. There seems little evidence for this other than the fact the film has been made by a group of Oxbridge-educated Notting Hill wealthy liberals. Many people have assumed he is based on Tony Blair. But it is obvious now that his *Love Actually* Prime Minister is a Tory. He is posh, wears a blue tie, and has just defeated the "other guy", the one who was "a poodle" to the US, i.e. Labour PM Tony Blair. It makes Grant's buffoonery easier to swallow, and the fact he wants to shag the tea lady almost before he's through the reception area on his first day at Downing Street almost obligatory. So much makes sense when you realise it; with a prescience of twenty-odd years, Hugh Grant is Boris Johnson.

4 Weeks to Christmas

Judy & John

Things have heated up on the set of the Judy and John Show, and Tony has now managed to get them both naked and in engaging in full-on simulated sex. Judy is on top, looking bored, John on his back, just as bored, Martin Freeman wondering where his career is to go next, probably not imagining it will be playing Bilbo Baggins in Peter Jackson's *Hobbit* trilogy.

It's still difficult to understand exactly what is going on here. Are they stand-ins? If so, this seems to have been going on a very long time. Over a week, if the on-screen text telling us we have now moved from five weeks before Christmas to four weeks before Christmas is anything to go by. But what really matters is that a connection is being made. John thanks Judy for being so easy to talk to. His English stiffness beginning to melt under the elongated glow of Judy's constantly referred-to nipples. Maybe it's because she's Welsh?

Colin

It's so weird that Tony is both director of big-budget movie with sex stand-ins, and mate of loser Colin. Or perhaps they are different Tonys, just played by the same actor. It is just so strange. Even stranger, if it is the same Tony, that Colin doesn't ever once ask him about his really interesting job (at least more interesting than serving canapés and delivering muffins). In fact, Colin never asks Tony a single thing about himself. Tony, a successful film director who would have gone to film school and worked extremely hard in an industry that had pretty much no black directors in 2003 – I mean, come on, Tony is a *pioneer*! – is only there to give Colin, a predatory sex pest, someone to talk about himself to. In this scene, Tony finds himself in Colin's white van, being told that Colin now has aspirations to become a sex tourist and has booked a flight to Wisconsin to have sex with loads of American girls he will find in bars. All we as viewers can hope for is that Richard Curtis doesn't send a camera crew to follow him there.

Harry & Mia

Harry the Boss is designating the organisation of the office Christmas party to Mia. Woman's work. He is a bit of a grouch, it has to be said. He asks Mia if she'll be bringing a boyfriend, which is about as unveiled a way of asking if she's single as you're ever likely to see. Mia replies, with the sultry glint of a cod begging to be battered, "I'll just be hanging around the mistletoe, waiting to be kissed." It's unsure here whether Harry the Boss ejaculates into his own pants, but Rickman's eyes narrow and his lips purse, similar to the way he did when Mary Elizabeth Mastrantonio's Maid Marian kneed him in the nuts in *Robin Hood: Prince of Thieves* (1991). But, of course, in that film, he was trying to rape her. It's all a bit gross.

Harry is a strange character. In this scene he shows himself to be completely unaware of the problem of sexual harassment in the workplace. Even from the perspective of 2003, it was clear to everyone that groping women is really not on. Yet here, Harry advises that the women avoid the office groper at the Christmas party, but there's no suggestion he will sit down with that particular member of staff for a pep talk on how not to sexually assault female members of staff, not in the same way he takes three minutes out of his day to tell Laura Linney's Sarah to shag Karl because frankly the way she pines after him is just sad and embarrassing. He does all this with a distinctly charmless sadsack harrumph.

But Love Is All Around. Mia wants him. Presumably because he wields some power. And presumably because he's Alan Rickman. We can all understand being attracted to Alan Rickman. One of my oldest friends, the playwright Siân Owen, still talks about the time she served Rickman in Piccadilly Waterstones when she worked there as a student as the greatest moment of her life. And she says this in front of her husband and kids. So again, here, Curtis quite cleverly trades on Rickman's star power and charisma, while taking no time or effort to create a likeable character for him. In fact, Harry the Boss is at best utterly reprehensible in his attitudes.[48] And yet we, the viewers, are supposed to sympathise with him. His behaviour will get much worse, and Rickman's star power will become even more valuable.

---

[48] As we'll see, I think the dynamic between Harry and his wife Karen is much more complicated than many give it credit for, but still, being a "classic fool" doesn't get Harry off the hook so easily.

Daniel & Karen

Emma Thompson continues to paper over the cracks of Curtis's horrible characterisations by being utterly charming as the increasingly grating Karen.[49] This is roughly one week since the burial of her best friend's wife, and still she finds it very difficult to act in an empathetic – or even sympathetic – way. Daniel expresses his concern that his eleven-year-old (step)son has barely left his bedroom. Karen's response seems to be that the boy is probably wanking, as he's at that age, ignoring the enormous grief he is processing up there. Daniel is worried his eleven-year-old is up injecting heroin into his eyeballs. Hyperbole, sure, but still begs the question if you're worried that he's harming himself, why not just open the door and go in; he's eleven. Thompson's character seems to be so far drawn with one thing in mind: to make her dismissive of things that are staring her right in the face. This will later explain the shock at her husband's affair.[50] So, Karen being so terse

---

[49] In 2020, the name "Karen" took on a symbolic meaning as an insult. Urban Dictionary explains it simply and effectively: "The stereotypical name associated with rude, obnoxious and insufferable middle-aged white women."

[50] Harry the Boss may not literally shag Mia, but it is only

and uncaring, so myopic and cold, is supposed to explain Harry the Boss's straying later on. It's partly her fault, you see, that her husband makes space in his life to bang his young secretary.

Still, Karen *is* awful. "I'm worried about my son being in his room all the time," says Daniel. "Don't worry about it," says Karen. "My teenage son – can't remember his name – is in his room all the time. Thank God." But his mother hasn't just died, has she? More's the pity.

They go to the kitchen for a cuppa, and Daniel finally gets his heart-to-heart with the "only person he can confide in", his best friend Karen. He breaks down. From Neeson, it's somewhere between a grimace and grin, but still we know it's a breakdown because his wife just died and he was just talking about how difficult it's going to be bringing up his stepson (that's right, Sam is his stepson, so that explains a little bit of the disconnect between them). Dry-crying, Neeson says, "Such a waste." Karen catches this, he no longer needs to put on a brave face; it's just the two of them, he has been so strong for so long. She puts her hand on his shoulder and says, "Get a grip. People hate sissies. No one's ever going to shag you if you cry all the time."

It's difficult to understand how this must have sounded funny on the page. 2003 was a very different time, and so much has changed, but still telling a grieving widower to stop being a sissy as nobody else will want to shag him seems a wildly misjudged joke. Perhaps Curtis felt he could weaponise the charms of Emma Thompson in order to pull it off. Or perhaps Curtis has forgotten, in the heat of the editing suite, it's been around eight minutes since we saw Daniel bury his wife.

---

circumstance that prevents it, and the way he deceives and manipulates Karen is exactly the stuff of full-blown affairs – he just happens to be found out before he manages to get Mia away for a dirty weekend in Margate.

Daniel & Sam

Daniel takes Sam to a bench overlooking the Thames, presumably to get him out of his heroin den bedroom,[51] and asks him if his isolated behaviour is to do with his mum dying a few weeks ago, or if there's something else, something more serious, going on? Daniel continues to treat the death of his wife, and Sam's mother, as if he has written off a car, albeit one that held a special place in his heart, like a collectable, or his first Audi. At this point any reasonable person would be screaming at the screen to give the kid a fucking break. His mum has just died. All he has is his stepdad, Liam Neeson, which is great if you get kidnapped and need rescuing by a man with a very particular set of skills, but less so if you need comfort or understanding that the death of a parent at that age is the collapsing of an entire universe. Scream with me at the screen, people. GIVE THE KID A BREAK.

---

[51] The deleted scenes on the *Love Actually* DVD reveal that it was neither heroin nor wanking that Sam was indulging in to assuage his grief during his bedroom isolation, but rather he was building a "shrine to love", bedecking his walls with posters from Baz Lurhmann's *Romeo + Juliet* (1996) and William Shakespeare's *Shakespeare in Love* (1998). I would suggest heroin and wanking would have been healthier.

But, wait. There is something. Sam has to admit it's not his mum dying. In fact, it is worse. He's in love. So, Emma Thompson was right, he has just been in his room wanking this whole time, his mother barely cold in her grave.

Daniel is relieved. Love. Thank God. Something he can talk to anyone about. Regardless of whether it's age appropriate. This is how they will bond, and hopefully Sam will not be put into a foster home. The problem is that Sam, here with his first lines of dialogue, is a precocious little shit, and describes "the total agony of love" as being the worst thing he could possibly imagine. His dead mother now slips from the image shown on the slide show at her funeral service, that of yummy mummy tragically cut down in her smiling-in-the-dusky-sunlight prime by the Big C, and now she feels more like Tilda Swinton drowning in motherhood in *We Need to Talk About Kevin* (2011), stopping in the street next to a pneumatic drill just to drown out the whiney little voice of Sam as he reads aloud *The Sorrows of Young Werther*. She was waiting for the sweet release of death, wasn't she? Not that anybody really cared.

Sarah & Karl

Laura Linney's in her office, and the lights are low so we know it's close of business; she's smacking on a bit of lippy so we also know she's got an eye on being proactive and pouncing on Enigmatic Karl, who's just across the way shutting down his computer for the night.

He says goodnight. He wears glasses, so he's not just a pretty face. She wears lipstick, so we know that she knows where he keeps the salami. Everything is set for the great meeting of bodies and minds. But he leaves. She missed her opportunity. What a waste of lippy.

We have also noticed that on her desk is the photo of a man. Is this Sarah's husband? Maybe she's a widow? After all, Curtis can have several cheating men in his film, but he's going to struggle to convince his audience that a cheating woman is anything other than a damnable slut. Unless she's Keira Knightley, who is allowed some mistakes at her age.

Sarah's phone goes. This is the second time we've seen her mobile ring, and she's a bit stressed at whatever is happening at the other end. The mystery builds. Who is calling her? Who is the man in the photo? Is Karl gay? (he has that nineties movie gay look; underwear model handsome with glasses).

Jamie

We're not in London anymore. Jamie, devasted by the betrayal of Jamie's Girlfriend, has run away to some villa in some European idyll in order to clear his head. Life is tough. He sits at a typewriter looking out over vineyards and valleys and says to himself, without another soul for a hundred miles to hear him, "Alone again. Naturally." We now know this is a man unlucky in love, and definitely not someone who invites people to treat him badly with his preponderance for self-pitying narcissism (and quoting Gilbert O'Sullivan). Of course, this is what Colin Firth does best, that flat-mouthed resilience, the depressed robot. This aspect of his skillset as an actor has been used to winning effect in many other roles, each of them very different but for their striking similarities. Mark Darcy in the *Bridget Jones* movies, a man who is so miserable and staid you are convinced for the first half of the first movie he is the villain of the piece. He won his Oscar for playing the royal so crippled with anxiety he can't bend his mouth out of that flat line in *The King's Speech* (2010). But he carries this single note off most successfully in Tom Ford's masterful adaptation of Christopher Isherwood's heartbreaking novel, *A Single Man* (2009). Here Firth does best what he does best, playing a man isolated in a crowded room. Richard Curtis was obviously attracted to this facet of Firth but decided to treat him to actual isolation in this otherwise overcrowded movie, and then still, it seems, gives him too many lines.

PM & Natalie

Lovely moment this, when the Prime Minister of the United Kingdom manipulates the power of his position to interrogate one of his office workers on her personal life, including whether she has a boyfriend or not, on the pretence of "getting to know" his staff a bit better. We establish here immediately that Natalie is from the dodgy end of Wandsworth, near a pub, the Queen's 'Ed, presumably because Curtis felt the Nag's 'Ed was a bit on the nose.[52] We are in a strange universe here, where a Tory PM finds himself the beneficiary of some work-placement scheme that puts rough-diamond working-class girls in the office of Number 10, and not the refined middle-class niece of a party donor on an unpaid internship. Must have been something that previous bunch of shits brought in. (Or maybe this is a Labour government, after all.) As the PM fishes for Natalie's current marital status, he makes a joke designed to cover his interrogation, and asks if she lives with her "three illegitimate but charming children?" At

---

[52] I am reliably informed by several sources (including the London-born and bred editor of this book) that Wandsworth doesn't really have a "dodgy end", suggesting again Curtis's limited understanding of the city he is always so associated with.

first you don't catch it, it's half-mumbled in that foppish bumble of Grant's that future PMs will turn into an electorate-conquering fine art. But yes, having played it back several times, it is clear he says the word "illegitimate". It's difficult to know where to start with this? The charmlessness of it, the sneer beneath that twinkling smile; the fact he is openly checking whether she has kids before he decides whether he's going to embark on an affair with her; the dismissive classism of it; the misogyny of it; the sheer creepiness of it; the fact that the PM, who has presumably just charmed the nation into voting him into the highest public office in the land, is incapable of a true human conversation with a woman he is attracted to, and has to initiate the false premise of a work situation, manipulating Natalie with his end of an extremely skewwhiff power dynamic. This whole scene, clearly meant to be charming and romantic and light and fluffy, is actually the PM interviewing Natalie for job of Chief Attendant to the Penis of the First Lord of the Treasury.

Natalie, of course, because this is written by a man, and a man who sees charm, sophistication and wit in a character like Grant's PM, finds this entire process charming, sophisticated and witty. At the end of the scene, Natalie having left the room, Grant, realising again he is falling hopelessly in love with his very own Eliza Doolittle, looks at a portrait of Margaret Thatcher on the wall and says, "Did you have this problem?" The joke here of course, as we all chug on our mugs of eggnog and throw our heads back in laughter, is that we all know Maggie's biggest problem was not falling for the intern, but was wondering if the guest bedroom had clean linen for when old friends like mass-murdering despot General Augusto Pinochet needed a place to stay while fleeing the courts of justice in his own native Chile.

Grant has a second punchline. "Of course, you did, you

saucy minx." The joke here is very sophisticated. Incongruity. Margaret Thatcher being notoriously allergic to condiments of all kinds, and so "saucy" is a wildly inappropriate word here. But secondly, Grant is betraying a basic honest truth about the power Thatcher held over her Cabinet, and party, of sexually repressed ex-public schoolboys: they all wanted to have sex with her. Richard Curtis, clearly understands this theory, something often referred to in Alan Clark, MP's famous diaries during his time as a junior minister in her government of the 1980s.[53] Tories saw (and see) in Thatcher both the sternness and coldness of the mother who couldn't love them and packed them off to boarding school at the earliest opportunity, and the sternness and coldness of the matron who took them on once they got there. Both roles are deeply intertwined with repressed Oedipal fantasies, ones that are perilously close to the surface for Grant's PM. Grant, it is obvious from this scene alone, is single because his sexual encounters are entirely dependent on strict power structures. He undoubtedly is riddled with self-loathing for his predilection for the servant class, while enduring a second helping of self-loathing for his inability to instigate sexual relations with older, more powerful women who remind him of his mother. This is a very, very complex and dark scene.[54]

---

[53] Clark, once described by colleague Dominic Lawson as "sleazy, vindictive, greedy, callous and cruel" and an "admirer of Hitler", drooled over the Iron Lady in his diaries, famously referring to her "lovely ankles". Many others have speculated on her mesmeric hold over her Cabinet of men.

[54] This is a reading taken by me without any research into the psychology of Freud, but having spent decades trying to figure out Tories.

Daniel & Sam

Daniel has decided the best way to salvage some kind of relationship with his stepson, now his wife (and the boy's mother) has been buried, is to help him sort out his love life. We establish Sam is not in love with another boy (Daniel carefully, like all good middle-class liberal dads, makes it clear it's fine if Sam is gay, but not preferable – but it's okay, phew, it's a girl); we also learn that the girl is the popular, heavenly one in school who everybody worships. Again, phew – the kid has taste. We also learn that it's quite likely the main problem with this entire unfolding storyline is that Sam, and the creepy-faced Thomas Brodie-Sangster who plays him, is just a little too young for all this. Eleven is too young for these conversations, too young for him to be so precocious, too young for his entire world not to be about his dead mother, and way too young for Liam Neeson to be saying "fuck" into his face as if he's a Russian kidnapper he's about to knife in the throat. If the kid had just been a few years older – make him thirteen or fourteen, and when Neeson says to him, "Basically, you're fucked" it wouldn't make you splutter into your Christmas cherry brandy.

3 Weeks to Christmas

Billy Mack & Ant & Dec

Billy Mack is on a very recognisable Saturday morning show (don't even try to figure out where that places us on the timeline of events) with the soon-to-be two most recognisable and award-laden television presenters in the country. That bloody song is blasting out again, and *Love Actually* is now moving so fast, and that song is playing so incessantly, the experience of watching it is akin to shopping in a depressed warehouse of knock-off price Christmas decorations.

Billy Mack is in a suit so shiny it might be greased tin foil. Ant and Dec look like they've been dressed by someone who had a rough night. It's revealed that Billy's main competition for the Christmas Number One will be boyband Blue, yet to embark on their duet with Elton John in real life (perhaps that was inspired by this rivalry with Billy Mack?).[55] Billy mentions he is annoyed that Blue weren't very nice about his record, which is a somewhat unhinged take, considering he himself has variously called it "crap" and "shit" on live interviews in the just the last seven

---

[55] Blue and Elton John collaborated on a hit re-recording of Elton's "Sorry Seems to Be the Hardest Word" in 2004.

days. Billy is flogging a line of marker pens or something, but it doesn't matter, it's just an excuse for him to write on a poster of Blue a speech bubble saying "We have small pricks" above them. So, apparently, *he* can be rude about his dreadful abomination of a record, but anybody else who does so will come in for childish humiliation at the hands of a washed-up old creep. He then reverts to calling himself "Uncle Billy" again as he addresses the kids watching and, presumably, the many actual children stood behind him making up the fake TV audience. He advises them to become pop stars, for the drugs. The man is a walking red flag. The climax of his spin-off movie would surely see Billy recuperating from a botched Operation Yewtree[56] investigation sunning himself on Jeffrey Epstein's yacht.

---

[56] Operation Yewtree, the 2012–15 Metropolitan Police investigation into paedophilia carried out by media personalities, most notably Jimmy Savile, will sadly largely be remembered as a succession of botch jobs, although in truth it led to several convictions.

Mark & Peter & Juliet

Turns out Mark is an art dealer, or gallery owner, or artist, or receptionist at a gallery, or someone who just walks in to galleries to use their phones. He is surrounded by art. Big blue breasts and bottoms, like Andy Warhol pastiches of a *Carry On...* movie, and schoolgirls pop in on their way home from St Trinians to giggle at them, which is no end of annoying for Mark who has adopted a peculiar semi-posh voice that sits in Andrew Lincoln's mouth like a cat turd he thought was a Christmas truffle. Peter is on the phone, calling from his office where he also rears pigeons (presumably, by the splodges of bird shit all over his shirt). He has a favour to ask, or rather Juliet has a favour to ask. He patches her through. The wedding video, it was a disaster, and as Mark had a camera on him all day, she wants to know if she can rescue some footage for her own documents. Mark is suspiciously reluctant. He's a bit rude about it too, in his cat-turd posh voice. Keira, of course, is beyond delightful and girly and smiley and fresh – even after her sadly short honeymoon (given the timeline of the movie).

Harry & Sarah & Mia

Harry the Boss is ragging on Sarah again about having sex with Enigmatic Karl. You may now start to wonder if he has a stake in this? Like, an office bet. Sarah's phone goes AGAIN, which means she will barely ever get to finish a conversation, never mind reach orgasm with the office hunk. The writing is on the wall, my friends.

Harry skittles over to Mia to ask about the Christmas party arrangements. She has found an art gallery as the venue (no doubt the one in which we just saw the blue boobs), a place, she says, full of dark corners for doing dark deeds. Just in case Harry is under the misapprehension Mia means murder, she shifts in her office chair a few inches, trying to expose her vulva. She means sex, or acts pertaining to sex, in a crotch-push the sexiness of which has not been seen since Ewan McGregor's drug-induced explosive diarrhoea in *Trainspotting* (1996). Harry seems almost terrified. Whatever that expression is on the face of one his generation's greatest actors, it definitely isn't arousal. Not even Alan Rickman could summon that look in the face of that vulva.

Mia turns back to her work, blissfully unaware at just how comically unattractive she has just made herself.

Jamie

Jamie is in his villa, rattling away on the typewriter, (because he is a writer from the 1950s who uses a typewriter), presumably working on his new Bellovian magnum opus about the betrayal of his ex with his brother. It becomes revealed here that Jamie, however, is not so much mourning the passing of *this* relationship with Jamie's Girlfriend, but is mourning the passing of *yet another* relationship. Eleonore, perhaps the property manager of the villa, asks if he has a "lady guest" like all the previous years he comes to this villa to write a novel. Nothing more romantic than taking a new girlfriend away to France for a few weeks so she can watch you write your novel.[57] And here comes the spanner in the works for Jamie. Eleanor has brought a cleaner, a Portuguese named Aurelia, played by Lúcia Moniz. The saving grace of this scene is that Firth has the chops to realise he can't fall in love at first sight. There is no spark, no lustful gaze. Firth is a gentleman, and as self-involved and self-pitying as all men of the gentleman class who have not been brow-beaten into sociopathy by the rigours of England's class system.

---

[57] As a novelist, I can testify this kind of arrangement is healthy neither for a novel or a relationship.

Jamie is charmingly bad in at least five languages. But he does try, which as every Englishman who has ever travelled abroad knows, is pretty much just as good as fluency. Jamie gives Aurelia a lift home after her shift scrubbing his toilet. It's awkward, so he attempts to bridge the language barrier with some Frankie Valli. Aurelia smiles. Firth is still showing no signs of any interest in Aurelia romantically or sexually. If this was the PM, he'd have drooled on to the steering wheel by now. But no, Firth is a smart cookie, and even though none of Curtis's dialogue in this scene is very funny, there's a real danger that Jamie may be coming off as the most admirable character in the movie so far, simply because he has not, as yet, tried to come on to the first pretty young woman who has crossed his path.

PM & POTUS

Billy Bob Thornton turns up as the President of the United States; a homely, southern, philandering slimeball. Thornton has the air of a man wondering what the giddy hell he's doing in this film. How did his career take this turn? His Oscar hangs around his neck like a phial of shame.[58] Natalie passes POTUS and the PM on the stairs. He ogles her, which is supposed to be offensive because this isn't English ogling, which is respectful and refined and welcomed, but American ogling, which is brash and sneery and frightening. "Did you see the pipes on that," POTUS confides to his bro, the PM, by which we can only infer that the President of the United States has the unusual fetish of being sexually attracted to women's vocal cords.[59]

Thornton's POTUS is obviously the villain of this narrative strand. This is emphasised when the PM walks in on him sniffing Natalie's hair, and she looks pleading at the PM as if to say, "This was not the type of inappropriate workplace sexual harassment I signed up for; I signed

---

[58] Thornton won an Oscar for Best Adapted Screenplay for *Sling Blade* in 1997.
[59] Research is inconclusive, but many reasonable people conclude "pipes" are actually "legs".

up for polite charming English sexual harassment, not this brash loud American sort." even though Thornton is actually playing this a bit reserved and snaky. The PM is livid, but doesn't show it, preferring instead to wait until the two world leaders are at a press conference to trot out some platitudes about the "special relationship". This is a great place to make a stand against a bully, of course. And a magical piece of international diplomacy.[60] The PM remains charming, cracking up the press corps and energising his staff by name dropping David Beckham and Harry Potter[61] when calling up the ranks of geniuses whose very existence demands Great Britain stand up to Billy Bob Thornton and his lecherous designs on Natalie.

---

[60] Less than a couple of decades later, this kind of fuck-you attitude finds a more damaging real-world form of expression in the Brexit vote.

[61] Very surprised he didn't namecheck Ant and Dec here. Although it worth noting that almost everything Curtis mentions here turns up in the 2012 London Olympics opening ceremony. Grant, indeed, reveals on the DVD commentary that the list originally included "Catherine Zeta-Jones's breasts" but he [Grant] felt this wasn't credible as a Prime Ministerial line.

PM & Karen

So, Karen, the worst best friend in history, is the PM's sister. Rachel to Grant's Boris. Only, so far, Rachel seems like she'd be far better company. She's called her brother up to ask what on earth he was thinking saying what he said about POTUS on that podium. Karen finds it hilarious of course, as if he's just gone a bit too far in a best man's speech. "I can't believe you just brought up that thing about the diplomatic incident. You're such a maverick, David." He blows her off, which is what they do in that family.

Harry & Karen

Oh dear. Harry the Boss is also Harry the Karen's Husband, and he's clearly not happy with his marriage. Otherwise why would he be spending so much time nagging on to Laura Linney about her sex life and flirting with his own secretary? Karen is blissfully unaware of the midlife crisis her husband is going through. They sit in an idyllic familial set-up, cosy lighting and warm jumpers, solitary pastimes undertaken in the vicinity of one another, that sort of thing. Joni Mitchell plays in the background, a harbinger of *Love Actually's* most famous scene, and the scene most offered up when it's being defended from people like me.

"Who is this?" asks Harry.

"Joni Mitchell," says Karen.

"I can't believe you're still listening to Joni Mitchell," Harry moans, revealing he has been unable to retain in his memory one of the most distinctive and popular singing voices of the last fifty years, despite his wife being a huge fan. This marriage is damned, and both participants damnable.

Karen points out that it was Joni Mitchell who taught her how to *feel*. Which on this evidence of this movie so far, makes Joni Mitchell damnable too.

PM

Peculiar voice cameo for Jo Whiley, perennial, and now veteran, mainstream radio DJ who has always done a very nice turn in inauthentic celebrity worship. She's playing a Girls Aloud cover of the Pointer Sisters' "Jump (for My Love)", and she's dedicating it to the PM.[62] This scene is notable for being the first time, thirty-six minutes in, that *Love Actually* makes me smile. The reason is that Hugh Grant, despite this turd of a role, remains a very good actor, and he is funny when dancing around the hallowed halls of Downing Street to "Jump (for My Love)", doing his dad disco moves, and getting caught out by his permanent secretary. It's good not just because Grant is good at bad dancing, but also because Richard Curtis has let him go, and hasn't put any execrable dialogue in his mouth.

---

[62] This Girls Aloud version was a Number Two hit single in the UK. The video has the band members intercut with the scene of Hugh Grant dancing around 10 Downing Street, made to look as if they're spying on him. I leave it to you as to whether you think *Love Actually* would have been improved had this been part of the film.

2 Weeks to Christmas

Jamie & Aurelia

Ah, the timeless comedy of language barriers. Colin Firth's Jamie remains somewhat affable, even if the depiction of the life of a writer is full of the romanticised clichés of privilege. But he's had a rough time, and he's throwing himself into his work, and whatever it is he writes, it obviously sells very well. Aurelia, however, getting quite comfortable in the presence of her new master, is already proving herself quite rude, telling Jamie, in Portuguese, that he doesn't understand, that he's getting chubbier every day.[63] Are we seeing the beginning of familiarity that could lead to romance here, or is this another depiction of the English wealthy class's arousal when being bossed around by the help?

Out by the lake, where Jamie is writing today without so much as a thought of a paperweight to stop the sheaves of typescript flying off out onto the water, a slight gust of wind blows his typescript out onto the water. Aurelia, the dutiful maid, sprints down the jetty. Jamie calls out to her that the book is trash, it's not worth it, like the self-pitying

---

[63] This will not be the last time *Love Actually* finds humour in the perception of a character's weight.

narcissist that he is, but it's no good, we're at the moment where the embers in Jamie's loins are rekindled, as Aurelia strips to her undies on the jetty in order to dive into the lake to save his terrible pages of tormented prose. The camera slows, the music swells to a swoon of sentimental strings, and Jamie stops his advance. Beneath the cardigan and tabard of the maid's uniform lies the body of a hot young woman. Jamie sees her differently now. And she has a back tattoo, not too big to be vulgar, but enough to inform Curtis's ideal audience that she probably has sex with men. The proverbial maid in the kitchen and tattooed slut in the bedroom. Good enough for our Jamie. Ladies and gentleman: we have Jamie's love strand.

Even in this moment of admiration of the female form/mild lechery, Firth refuses to allow Jamie to become too leery, too lip-smacking. He jumps/falls in to the lake after Aurelia, and explains again, as his toes are nibbled by eels, that the book is not worth it. It's hardly Shakespeare. Or Harry Potter. Or David Beckham's right boot, for that matter.

Back at the villa, the two dry off, and Jamie makes a hot bevvy. He, and we, see Aurelia differently now, because her naked shoulder is showing, and her hair is wet. She is a person, not just a maid, and maybe… just maybe… Jamie can save her from a life of servitude, and in the process save himself.

YES.

BOOM!

Curtis is on fire in this scene.

As they try to navigate the language barrier, we discover Jamie is in fact a writer of crime thrillers. His references to how bad his writing is belies a common snobbery in the literary classes, who believe genre fiction to be a rung or two below "literary fiction" on the ladder of life. His self-loathing, then, could be due to his falling in with the genre crowd, when his youthful aspirations were more "respectful". There's a half-interesting story here. One that will go no further. Because now we also discover – because time and nuanced character development wait for no man in *Love Actually* – that he is already in love with Aurelia, and she with him. They just don't know how to tell each other. Only they do tell each other, in languages they know the other cannot understand. A clever trick, and one that suggests the Jamie–Aurelia story thread, although shadowed like others with the imbalance in the power dynamic between the man and the woman, is perhaps the strand Curtis is most invested in, emotionally and creatively.

It's a shame then, that Aurelia looks so much younger than Jamie, something that's very apparent here as they clumsily part ways, and then right after as he drives her home, and she looks very much like the babysitter his wife hired and with whom he's about to start a torrid backseat love affair.

Mark & Juliet

Breakfast, and Mark is shovelling Frosties into his mouth while watching the new video for Billy Mack's Christmas record, in which Mack seems to have created a festive homage to Robert Palmer's famous "Addicted to Love" video. Mack licks his fingers into the camera, kind of like a Leslie Grantham[64] sex video only with slightly less star power. Mark finds this funny. The TV presenter refers to Billy Mack as the "Bad Grandad of rock 'n' roll" which, in a strange way, sums up perfectly what the music business thinks of rock 'n' roll.

Doorbell. It's Juliet. Oh bugger. Mark has been horrible to her, trying and keep her at arm's length from his love for her. But she's just so bloody chirpy and persistently ignorant of his twatishness, she's turned up, at breakfast time, with some banoffee pie to try and win him over into friendship.[65] She has an ulterior motive, though. She wants that

---

[64] For over twenty years, on and off, Leslie Grantham played British television soap's premier bad guy, Dirty Den Watts in *Eastenders*. His stint on the show finally ended in scandal in 2004 when he was filmed "sucking his own finger in a sexual manner" to an undercover "reporter".

[65] Breakfast banoffee pie must be a London thing.

bloody wedding video, as well as to secure Mark's friendship. Mark can't find it, he says, but she finds it easily on his shelf next to a VHS copy of *Rear Window*, and probably *The Godfather* and *Pulp Fiction*, and other movies boys like to explain to girls at parties.

Mark is in the shit now, as he knows something Juliet doesn't: that he's a twat and he's essentially made a wankbank video of her on her wedding day. This will be embarrassing. But wait... this is the height of romance. That's how this will play out. A tragedy. He is lovesick, and there is nothing he can do about it. Juliet clocks that the video is of her, almost exclusively in close up, in some horrifying Ballardian camcorder sex-act entanglement. Mark is rumbled, admits as much, and runs out into the street where the deathless emotional marker of a Dido[66] record awaits him.

Some classy turmoil acting here from Lincoln, who must have brought a proud smile to the face of his turmoil acting coach at RADA where Lincoln changed his name to Lincoln from Clutterbuck, a name strangely close to the word clusterfuck, which is, ironically, the perfect one-word review of *Love Actually*.

---

[66] *No Angel*, the 1999 debut album by Dido Florian Cloud de Bouneville O'Malley Armstrong, quickly became the soundtrack of English white middle-class mediocrity.

PM & Annie

We haven't really talked about Annie before, played by Nina Sosanya, because she's one of the actors who fill up the non-love strand character bank in *Love Actually* (sometimes known as the supporting cast). This is the first time she has any role other than introducing the PM to another character or telling him he's fabulous or telling him he has a phone call. The PM, aware there is a problem with his attraction to Natalie, asks Annie if she can "redistribute" Natalie. This apparently isn't mafia speak for chopping up a person and dropping their limbs into different corners of the city. He wants Natalie moved to another department, physically intact, so for a moment we must be concerned he has slept with her, as we have already established that would be the correct system of things. And nothing really suggests he hasn't. But Annie reveals herself here to have the mind of a middle-aged white man, when she refers to Natalie as the one with the massive arse and huge thighs. The way she objectifies Natalie and refers to her as "plump" is a jarring moment of casual misogyny that confirms the prejudices of the film, as well as the dumbheadedness of the characters. Why does Annie speak this way, in such bullying, cruel, misogynistic language? Well, she doesn't, does she? Richard Curtis does.[67]

---

[67] The presence of Nina Sosanya, a prolific and extremely watchable TV star, raises the question whether *Love Actually*, were it made today, be far more successful as a television serial. The attitude to TV from the feature film fraternity of actors and directors in 2003 was very different to what it is now, and it's doubtful many of the actors of *Love Actually* would have signed up to a mini-series. But now, of course, the landscape is greatly changed. Perhaps a slightly less misogynistic attitude in the script, and more space to develop characters, could produce a serial as enjoyable as *Love Actually* already thinks it is.

Daniel & Sam

Daniel is still moping over his dead wife, which must be getting right on Karen's tits by now. He is staring at his wife Joanna's[68] photo on his desk. Sissy. Sam comes in, looking like a dying Victorian child, in his dressing gown, and tells Daniel that the girl he loves, Joanna, is leaving and going back to her real home in America. Yes, you caught that; weirdly, Richard Curtis has decided to name both Sam's dead mother and his unrequited love Joanna.[69] Daniel doesn't make the connection, even though it's screaming at him to do so. The eleven-year-old is lusting after a girl with the same name as his dead mother. Don't you think you

---
[68] Daniel's dead wife gets a name, but I missed when this was. Sorry.
[69] A deleted scene on the *Love Actually* DVD goes some way to explain this decision (although not really); it is an excuse, as Curtis himself explains, for Liam Neeson to mime to Scott Walker's "Joanna". Noting the names are the same, Daniel sees this as "spooky" but decides it's a point over which he and Sam can bond. Also worth noting, perhaps, is that Curtis refers to Scott Walker, a musical hero of his, as "the great 1960s singer", ignoring Walker's subsequent three-decades-long career as a leading and widely influential avant-garde composer and recording artist, almost as if he doesn't know Walker did any of that difficult stuff.

should talk to him about this, Daniel? Maybe Sam could talk to a professional, just to help him through these difficult times? But no, Daniel's solution to this Freudian minefield is to sit Sam down in front of a screening of *Titanic* (1997), James Cameron's hideously schmaltzy, all-conquering romantic tragedy.[70] Yes, I haven't been able to figure out the line of thinking there either. But it gives Daniel the platform for a pep talk. There's more fish in the sea, Daniel says. Perhaps that's why he's put *Titanic* on. Lots of sea in that movie. There's more than one person out there for you, Sam, he says. I'm actually already being encouraged to shag around a bit, now we've buried your mum and all that. My friend Karen says I could be up to my neck in women as soon as I stop crying.

---

[70] Carl Wilson's analysis of *Titanic* in *Let's Talk About Love* is the final word on the matter.

PM

A solemn scene. The PM, shuffling through papers like all good PMs do, is feeling the consequences of his decision to have Natalie "redistributed". A different woman, older, well spoken (although we'll leave it to Annie to judge whether she's plumper than Natalie or not), brings the PM his cuppa. It's just all so bloody sad.

Jamie & Aurelia

Jamie's off; filling the boot of his car with booze and garlic, Christmas presents for the people back home. His time away has been productive. His novel may have blown into a lake, but his heart is at least partially mended by the experience of meeting Aurelia, finally a woman who can understand him (apart from the fact she can't literally understand him, because of the language barrier etc. etc. A barrier that continues to hamper their romantic union, even at this pivotal goodbye moment). Aurelia still is going for the pigtail-pulling strategy – she doesn't care whether he can understand her or not – taking the piss out of Jamie's slow typing and bad driving. It's a defence mechanism, as Mark would easily identify; she's trying to keep him at arm's length, or something. They are parting company, Master and Maid, and may never see each other again.

And here we have the first kiss, one hour and two minutes into *Love Actually*. It's a bold move, not least because he is her boss, and because she has no idea how he feels about her, and because he's just dropped her off on the hard shoulder of a motorway, which, without the soft comfort of a lingual explanation, one could reasonably assume was an aggressive note of rejection.

He watches her walk away.

Billy Mack

Another quick view of Billy Mack's Robert Palmer video; it flashes up on to the screen with much the same effect of the hell scenes from space horror *Event Horizon* (1997).[71] Billy Mack contorts and twists in what one must assume is Bill Nighy's impression of a rock singer, and not that his shirt has been poisoned like in some Greek tragedy.[72]

Apart from the hideous contortions of Mack, the video is very tasteful, with close-ups of heaving bosoms and the tongues of band members slathering seductively over glistening rouged lips.

---

[71] Paul W. S. Anderson's sci-fi horror film is remembered as an overlooked classic by many but is in fact a fairly rushed slasher B-movie that does little with the tropes of the genre. The reason it has made such an indelible mark in the minds of a generation is the hyper-gory flash-frame found footage of the hellish fate of the movie's lost interstellar explorers. Those two segments of that film are arguably some of the most effective seconds in horror movie history.

[72] Several times during the hours involved in this forensic examination of *Love Actually*, my mind drifted to the merciless brutality of Greek revenge. At one point I even looked to see if a poisoned dress, such as the one Euripides's Medea sends to the new wife of Jason, her ex, was available to buy online.

Sam & Daniel

As any parent would hope, Sam is watching Billy Mack's video through the window of a high-street store. It's given him ideas. But not that Daniel was right about the fish-in-the-sea thing, but rather that he must rush home immediately to tell Daniel the way to win over the heart of Joanna (the girl he fancies in school, not his dead mum) is to become a musician. Or rather, a drummer (which, as all musicians know, is *not* the same thing). So, here we have some proof that Billy Mack's advice to kiddies from "Uncle Billy" may actually have some traction. Okay, so Sam hasn't decided to chase rock 'n' roll stardom in the pursuit of free narcotics, as Mack advised on the Ant 'n' Dec Show, but the message of musician = fanny magnet has clearly made it through via the power of television. This also raises the question of whether the Billy Mack video is really as lascivious as we have just seen, or whether we have just witnessed a heightened narrowed version through the eyes of a fucked-up uber-hormonal eleven-year-old kid trying to process the death of his mother by chasing a girl in school with the same name. This idea opens up a whole can of worms, asking us to view the film as a potential surrealist experiment in the distortions of reality brought about by the intense emotional states experienced during love/grief/trauma/elation/puberty. Regardless of how we're meant to watch this, there is still no excuse for the way Neeson talks to his eleven-year-old stepson. "Girls love musicians. Even the weird ones," says Sam. "That's right," says Neeson; "Even Meat Loaf got laid at least once."[73] Sam doesn't understand, not least because only Americans and bad writers use the word "laid", but also because it must be becoming increasingly difficult for Sam not to call up the social workers himself and be asked to be housed in foster care, at least until Daniel has finished with his breakdown.

But here is a major plot point. Sam has decided the way to win the heart of Joanna (not his dead mother) is to learn the drums and play in the band of the school Christmas concert. Here we are presented with the climax toward which *Love Actually* will now work. The Christmas Concert. A place for our disparate array of characters to converge, and for loose ends to be tied up, and for our glasses of sherry to be clinked and our tears of festive joy to be wiped from our eyes. The Christmas Concert, where *Love Actually* will win out.

---

[73] The singer's name, as he occasionally points out in interviews, is correctly written as two words, which is why *The New York Times* calls him "Mr Loaf". Incidentally, is this yet another example of the film's obsessive fat shaming?

Sarah

Sarah, with a fading gleam of pride, puts the saddest, smallest Christmas tree on a shelf in her flat. There is no point to this scene other than to show just how sad and fucking lonely she is.

Office Christmas Party

A big ensemble scene, in which a great many plots will lurch forward. It's time, after all, for something to start happening.

But first: boobs.[74]

Sarah is alone at the party, hoping nobody will notice she is alone with a drink standing right in front of a row of men's arses. It's all she can do to stop herself from licking them. Harry the Boss and Karen are there, of course, and the moment Karen's back is turned, Mia rises up as if from the pits of Hell, in a red flag of a red dress, complete with little devil horns, strange both because it is neither Halloween nor is it a fancy dress party. So, she just has some horns on. Unless... surely not... this is a visual signifier of her seductive intentions toward Harry the Boss? Surely

---

[74] It's not easy, as the film goes on, to truly understand why the exhibits at Mark's gallery are so lurid. It must be funny. Boobs and bums. Must be funny. It's a shame there are no paintings of farts. The only thing even funnier than boobs and bums. There are several deleted scenes, available to watch on the DVD if you're so inclined, that give more screen time to the hilarity of boobs and bums at this exhibition, without ever really doing much more than that.

not. I mean, his wife's right there. She must be more subtle than that. Mia wants to dance. Harry says okay then, which seems a dangerously precarious position to put yourself in with the horny devil given the proximity of his wife, Karen. We see Mark is there, dancing, looking across at Mia with the eyes of someone who has already danced with the devil. He seems a little jealous, but surely not, as he's in love with Keira Knightley, so his glances over to Mia and Harry must be the glances of a man cursed with the Cassandrian gift of predicting impending doom. Mia and Harry go for a close, slow dance, in full view of Karen. What we know of Karen so far leads us to be less than surprised her emotions haven't been prickled by the sight of her husband pressed up against his secretary to the sound of Kelly Clarkson. Mark, presumably, is watching from the side with the fixed gaze of someone who is watching a car crash happen but is powerless to do anything about it. Harry tells Mia she looks pretty, which must feel a soft response considering the amount of effort Mia is putting in at the moment. Mia whispers into Harry's ear, "It's all for you," which is eerily reminiscent of the line from Damien's nanny just before she performatively hangs herself at the birthday party in *The Omen* (1976).

PM

Quick scene where the PM, still lonely and alone and lonesome and a loner, is leafing through some important government documents while Billy Mack exposes his penis to Michael Parkinson (the *real* Michael Parkinson) on TV. The PM laughs, because it reminds him of his Bullingdon Club days assaulting waitresses in Oxford. But this just reminds him how much he's missing Natalie.

Office Christmas Party

Harry the Boss is still deep in convo with Mia. Karen watches on, as if going over there and interrupting her husband's seduction might be intruding. And then perhaps the most unlikely thing happens. Enigmatic Karl pops up, like a Muppet, and asks Sarah if she'd like to dance. It's all a bit Senior Prom, but she nervously says yes, and they go out to get jiggy to Justin Timberlake. Unfortunately, their plans to take it slow are well and truly scuppered when the DJ, making a decision to go down in the annals of irrational DJing decisions, scratches off Timberlake for Norah Jones's "Turn Me On". They are now obliged to slow dance. There is now no avoiding Love. An office crush on Enigmatic Karl is now full-blown love between them both, complete with Norah Jones, and Enigmatic Karl closing his eyes and sniffing Sarah's hair, which as we all know is the universal sign for either *Love* or *Serial Killer Chooses Next Victim*.

Before the record has even finished, they get in Enigmatic Karl's car and off they rush, panting, back to Sarah's place and her sad little fibre optic Christmas tree. Enigmatic Karl can drive, of course, because he is too enigmatic to allow himself to drink at the office Christmas party.

Sarah & Karl

Laura Linney remains the shining light of this movie. She is sincere, funny, and charming, and it's a damn shame she doesn't eventually get together with Colin Firth's Jamie, who could do with someone with Sarah's baggage to snap him out of his self-loathing narcissism. But she's going for the enigma that is Enigmatic Karl – and frankly at this point I can't remember if Jamie and Sarah might be related or something.

Sarah and Enigmatic Karl are going to get it on. Norah Jones has already told them how they feel about each other. I love in this scene how one light switch by the front door turns on every light in Sarah's apartment. That is some pretty bold leccy fittings her landlord has had put in. But I admit that's probably not the focus of this scene for most people. Sarah and Karl are about to do sex, just five minutes after the film's first kiss. It's all getting quite heated here. It's all going well. They're getting naked. Eva Cassidy is playing, which is the sex soundtrack of all couples in Notting Hill.

And then a phone rings.

Ah yes. Sarah's always taking calls on her Nokia, and there's a mystery to the frequency and inconvenience of these calls. Astride Enigmatic Karl, she takes the call. Enigmatic Karl, becoming less enigmatic by the second, is a bit miffed. Granted, the call could be very important, and he knows nothing about Sarah's life, her responsibilities, or what the phone ringing might mean; but his eyes say, seriously, this is going to take two minutes. Tops. We learn here that her brother in not well and that he calls *a lot*. He needs an exorcist, like all people with mental health issues do from to time. The Pope? Or Jon Bon Jovi? "Are we done with the cheap jokes that use mental health problems as a punchline?" Enigmatic Karl is thinking. "I have a dying erection." But the buzz is killed. Oh shit, she wants to talk about her mad brother. Karl is understanding. Nods. Grabs her. Takes up where they left off. He is being enigmatic again. The phone rings in that way they used to do before people became embarrassed by the sound of a Nokia ringtone. This time Karl is less understanding. Not enigmatic at all. He's bordering on a stereotype of male entitlement. This, his eyes now say, is a fucking drag. Sarah says down the phone that she will be right there. The sex is on hold. Maybe permanently. She has a mental brother after all, and both Eva Cassidy and Norah Jones have checked out too. Mark this down as a bad experience, Karl. Get out of there while you still can, is the message here. He sits on the bed in his pants, Sarah on the floor in her slip. It's like a Caravaggio painting.

Harry & Karen

In the bedroom, after the party, Karen, solemnly, mentions how she's getting old, how she's getting fat, and then, almost apologetically, says to Harry that Mia is pretty, the word feeling more sincere in Karen's mouth than it ever did in Harry's. Harry reclines on the bed, knowing his only defence is to play dumb. You know I know she's pretty, and I know you know I know, and you know I know you know I'm pretending I haven't noticed. Alan Rickman, by this point, looks positively reptilian, and you realise he's looked narrow-eyed the entire film; he looks puffy, tired, lacking in both the vim and the vigour that made him an international star in *Die Hard* (1988) and *Robin Hood: Prince of Thieves* (1991), and would make him a favourite of another generation of kids as Professor Snape in the Harry Potter movies. No, he has no energy in this role. And it's hardly surprising. Who is Harry? He's a boss and a husband. We know nothing of his business, nothing of his family, we know he doesn't recognise who Joni Mitchell is, but apart from that all we really know is he's tired, maybe a bit depressed, and heading toward a disastrous, not-so-secret office affair with his secretary.

Mia

Mia strips to her underwear. Not sure why we need to see that.

Sarah & Her Brother

Structurally, we are now in the low–centre point of the film, where we will have no jokes, and the soundtrack will be in the minor key. After Harry is warned off his secretary by his wife, and Mia is seen to have wasted her scarlet lingerie on a night alone in bed, we see Sarah visiting her violently mentally ill brother, Michael, in an institution. Michael, however, is from another movie, because he is played with a striking realism by Michael Fitzgerald, overweight and sweaty, his eyes flickering with danger; he is at odds with the tone of the film he finds himself in. There is so much going unexplained here. Why are the two of them in the UK, Americans without much money, and Michael with a debilitating mental health condition that renders him institutionalised? The institution he is retired in is a strange place. A place that allows him to call his stressed-out sister at any time of the day or night to play out his schizophrenic fantasies down the line, a place that leaves him to take a swipe at her with a forearm that looks like it could fell a tree, before restraining him, watching him return to calm, and then leaving him to do it again. Is it possible that Richard Curtis simply required some hook on which to hang this central tonal downturn, and has reached out to mental illness, and has done so without any real knowledge of it, or the systems that work to serve those afflicted with it?

Harry & Karen

In bed now. Karen can't sleep. Mia is a threat. Has Karen pushed Harry away with her incessant playing of Joni Mitchell?

Harry & Mia

Next morning (because we seem to have hit the rails of an actual timeline here), and we're back in the office. Harry is off to do some Christmas shopping. Mia asks, with that vixen's glare she's been practising in the mirror, if he is going to get her a gift. Doubtful, it says on his face. See you later, Harry says, clearly slightly worried he might actually be having an affair. Mia leans her chin on her hands. It's not sexy, it's a bit weird. "Looking forward to it," she purrs. "A lot." Harry scarpers, terrified. But as soon as he's made it to Selfridges, he calls Mia, who is now coquettishly curled in her office chair like a Cheshire cat curling the phone cable around her finger as if it's a BDSM tourniquet. Harry has decided to openly flirt with her by asking if she wants some office stationery. This is the moment where you realise Karen, his wife, has lost interest in him because he is a complete dick. He doesn't even have the imagination or energy to truly engage in this affair. And the truth is, neither does Rickman.

Harry & Karen

For the time being, we appear to have abandoned all other storylines while we sort out Harry and Karen's marriage. Karen is meeting her husband for a Christmas shopping spree.[75] Harry is going to get himself in a bit of a pickle here, because he's kind of committed himself to getting Mia a present, and there's definitely no way he's going to make a separate shopping trip, oh no. He doesn't have the energy for that kind of malarkey. So, he's going to just give Karen the slip and quickly shove a stapler in his pocket or something, just to prove to Mia that he is indeed pleased to see her.

---

[75] We all know that mums don't do Christmas "shopping sprees"; they do slogs, with arms and shoulders weighed down by bouquets of overflowing bags. Emma Thompson gives Karen the perfect shuffling feet of this kind of mum, not energised by Christmas, but driven forward by the gruelling satisfaction of ticking chores off a list.

Harry & Rufus

A comedic set piece that stands as a highlight of the film. That's why so much stock is put on the cameo, and the comedy genius, of old friend of Richard Curtis, Rowan Atkinson. Here, Atkinson, as a retail assistant, takes so long to gift-wrap the necklace Harry has impulsively decided to buy for Mia, that he ends up unable get it done before Karen shows up. It's a masterclass in casually built tension and stands out from the laziness of much of the rest of *Love Actually*'s set pieces. Watching Atkinson build the tension in this rudimentary offering is like watching Picasso draw a stickman on a napkin, but that doesn't mean there won't be distinct and enjoyable flourishes in that stickman. Rickman goes to some lengths to emphasise just what a bloated, lizardy old sap Harry is, while Atkinson delicately navigates the thinness of his duties, plinking several accoutrements into the gift bag of the expensive necklace Harry took all of 1.5 seconds picking for Mia. One has to wonder what exactly it is Harry is looking for in this affair of his? There is clearly no thrill in the chase. He spends this moment looking like a dildo whose batteries are draining.[76]

That's all we see of Rufus, which is hardly surprising, as Atkinson doesn't need the cash or the exposure of *Love Actually*, being a global megastar after the success of *Mr Bean* (1997).[77]

And this marks the end of the downbeat central section.

---

[76] In a bizarre and very welcome revelation, Emma Freud, *Love Actually* script editor and wife of Richard Curtis, revealed on Twitter in 2016 that Rowan Atkinson's Rufus was originally supposed to be an angel, sent to earth to scupper Harry's plans to buy Mia an expensive necklace. Had the makers of *Love Actually* stuck to this heavenly storyline, it might have given some real magic to a film where many people feel they see magic, when in fact there is none.

[77] *Mr Bean* grossed $250 million worldwide, profiting considerably on its $18 million budget.

1 Week to Christmas

As the climax gets ever, slowly, closer, we are treated to a fast-paced edit of a montage of scenes, to the soundtrack of the great Darlene Love and Bruce Springsteen's E-Street Band doing "All Alone on Christmas", a song that can only ever heighten an experience.

Colin

Oh. I'd almost forgotten about Colin. A face guaranteed to diminish any experience. He's rented out his flat to pay for his plane ticket to America, which also means he owns his own flat in London. Colin does. Colin, who serves canapés and delivers muffins. His background, his life, just became much more interesting.

Judy & John

Again, Curtis has decided to cut directly from Tony, just seen answering the door to Colin and providing foil for Colin's exposition, to Tony, now directing a simulated blow job on set of this sex-filled mainstream movie he's directing. This cavalier attitude to what story Tony is in, and when, proves a dizzying viewing experience.

John takes this opportunity, while Judy's head moves back and forth from his crotch like a mechanical woodpecker, to ask her if she'd like to go for a Christmas drink. The incongruity of the question to the circumstances is, of course, hilarious. Cut to John doing his best bashful Martin Freeman impression, on his back, Judy's thighs in a position suggesting she is sitting on his chest. We have to hope this unorthodox sexual position, which presumably somehow has to fit into the narrative of a mainstream, and not pornographic, movie (because they are stand-ins, and not adult actors), is not the moment where the female character is doing a poo on the male character.[78]

---

[78] This is not to cast judgement or seem prudish; I just haven't been able to understand the context that this camera angle suggests for this movie-within-a-movie.

Karen & Harry

Harry has been out, and Karen meets him at the door like the dutiful wife, to take his coat and hang it up. She feels the weight of his coat, and, as Harry goes into the house harrumphing and grumbling with his reptilian glare, Karen discovers in his coat pocket an expensive necklace. Oh dear, Harry, you silly, silly sausage. Thinking Harry has thrown off the shackles of his midlife crisis, Karen is sure the gift is for her. No scarf this year, oh no! But a £270 necklace from Selfridges. Something has put lead in Harry's pencil. Maybe it was that Joni Mitchell record she had on at breakfast?

In the living room, Harry and Karen's children, who we can be forgiven for having forgot existed, and maybe even have a bit of a double take at how young these interlopers seem to be, are performing – or practising a performance – of the nativity. This brief moment presents the viewer with perhaps the only truly charming moment of the entire of *Love Actually*, when, ignoring the fact that Karen thinks Jesus was born in Jerusalem and not Bethlehem, we see the kids have cast Barney the Dinosaur in the role of Baby Jesus. Awwwwww.

Jamie

Montage continues. Jamie is learning Portuguese. Worry not, Aurelia, he will be back to pick you up from that motorway lay-by very soon.

Karen

Shit, Karen's totally got her hopes up that necklace is for her.

Colin

Colin is off. Convinced that sexual intercourse is waiting for him in America. He lands in Milwaukee and the soundtrack swaps abruptly to Carlos Santana.[79] It is a choice of record designed to signify that we are now in America, but of all the songs in the history of rock 'n' roll to have chosen, it seems lazy to have chosen a distinctly Latino record to symbolise entry to a state that in the 2000 US census registered as 3% Hispanic. Santana's "Smooth"[80] doesn't speak of snow and clipped midwestern accents. It speaks of tequila and sun-drenched parties and Rob Thomas not quite being able to figure out why life has afforded him such distinction.

There are many other strange errors in this scene. Wisconsin is a Miller state (they are fiercely proud of their home-state brew), not a Budweiser one, which Colin orders; and the walls of the bar are adorned with banners of sports teams from other parts of America. Lazy? Probably. But also,

---

[79] More precisely, his megahit with Matchbox Twenty's Rob Thomas, a record that incontrovertibly speaks of the awfulness of this period in American musical history.
[80] In 2018, "Smooth" was ranked by *Billboard* as the second most successful single of all time.

something else is about to happen. Sex tourist and future serial killer Colin, it turns out, was right all along. American women fall at his feet because of his accent. He has been in America for half an hour and it appears like he is going to be invited to his own private supermodel orgy, just because of the way he ordered a beer. There is no humour in this, because it is so absurd, not to mention offensive to women (of America, but also any nation). So, how does this stack up? The only answer is to return to the serial killer idea (remember that idea I had a thousand hours ago?), and this phase of his evolution into the man who will terrorise London in ten years or so until DCI John Luther takes him down. This phase is his *American Psycho* phase, and more precisely, the Mary Harron interpretation of the *American Psycho* story.[81] Colin is delusional, and we are watching his delusion through his eyes. Is any of this true? That he owns his own flat? That he flies to Milwaukee? That he goes to a bar and orders a Budweiser, the beer all dickheads would imagine ordering if they went to a bar in Randomsville, USA? That he immediately is chatted up by Ivana Milićević, a teenage boy's vision of what a beautiful woman looks like (no offence to Ivana Milićević)? Add to that January Jones (yet to marry Don Draper) and Elisha Cuthbert (a huge star at the time due to her concurrent role as Jack Bauer's daughter in *24*), and you have the ultimate sex tourist fantasia of the mind of a disturbed male human, who in reality has passed out from oxygen deprivation in a rented London basement where the air stings from the smell of masturbatory excess.

---

[81] Mary Harron directed the 2000 film adaptation of the Bret Easton Ellis novel, where she emphasises the ambiguity of "serial killer" Patrick Bateman's delusions, so that by the end of the film, the viewer cannot be sure if the brutal sadistic murders that have occurred in the last ninety minutes of screen time didn't all just happen inside Bateman's head. Perhaps the most brutal and caustic statement on toxic masculinity cinema has yet to see.

Karen & Harry

The scene. The one that chokes people up, preparing them for the deluge of sympathetic tears to come in the next scene. Emma Thompson, finally given something interesting to do as Karen, plays the moment very well, of course. Harry is a massive shit. Karen is devastated. She won't be getting the £270 necklace, but a crappy old Joni Mitchell CD. The world collapses.

But let's take an alternative reading of this. Harry the Boss, let's not mess about, has done an appalling thing, and is appalling in his half-hearted, harrumphing deceptions. But he is a fairly inert presence.[82] Curtis has decided to make Mia the pursuant, the controller of the

---

[82] Emma Freud, in another Twitter revelation, stated categorically that Harry and Mia *did* consummate their affair. This seems unfair, both to the characters and viewers, as the ambiguity of this relationship is what gives people enough wiggle room when judging Harry, Mia, and, let's be honest, Karen. Anybody who has seen the documentary *Hilary* (2019), about Hilary Clinton, will be reminded of how society judges women who stand by their man. That Harry and Mia had sex off screen makes a big difference to how we perceive the reactions of the characters. It also raises the question as to whether Karen herself is fully aware of the whole story, just like the audience isn't.

burgeoning affair. He wasn't even going to get her a present. She demanded one. What is it he got her? An expensive shiny thing it took him a micro-glance to choose. As with everything in life, Harry is going through the motions, hurtling toward retirement, his armchair, and then death, hardly able to believe life has even happened to him. The necklace is a symbol for just how ill-matched Harry is to even the notion of an affair. He isn't interested in it. What he is, is a man used to being pushed from one unsatisfying human encounter to the next, and there is more of an air about him of a man who thinks it is expected of him to have an affair with Mia. Not once does he look the slightest bit interested in Mia. It all seems a bit of a chore. The only thing he's ever had going for him in his life is his wife. Karen. They have been long married, and complacency has found its way in. But when it comes down to it, he didn't just buy Karen a cheap bit of plastic, he bought her the latest Joni Mitchell album, an artistic statement by a woman Karen earlier said was the person who *taught her how to feel*. Let that sink in for a moment. How to *feel*. He has thought about this, not just made an effort to get her something she would appreciate, but he has made an effort to correct himself on his lack of attention to Joni Mitchell's music and his wife's devotion to her output. On top of this, *Both Sides Now* (2000), the album he has bought for her, is a painfully romantic record. Harry may not have known that, but it's just as likely he's investigated by reading reviews, all of which at that time point to the fact it is a concept album about the journey of loving relationships. In the liner notes, Larry Klein, who co-produced the album, writes that *Both Sides Now* is "a programmatic suite documenting a relationship from initial flirtation through optimistic consummation, metamorphosing into disillusionment, ironic despair, and finally resolving in the philosophical overview of acceptance and the probability of the cycle repeating itself". Is Richard Curtis aware of this, or has he just picked an album a middle-aged woman might like? Well, if he *is* aware of the symbolism of *Both Sides Now*, and the richness it provides this scene, then it shows an attention to subtextual sophistication that is strikingly absent from the rest of the movie.

Most fans view this scene as the moment Karen realises she is betrayed, and that it is a typical story of a shitty bored husband banging his young hot secretary. But it is nothing of the sort. It is the moment when a man trapped by his own depression and mediocrity tries to cry out to his wife, he's telling her he loves her, and that he doesn't know why he's such a dick. It's something hardwired into the man who is befuddled by his own lack of imagination and energy. He may sound like an arrogant, condescending smart-arse when he says the gift is to "continue her emotional education", but he is actually trying to be cute, explaining that he has listened to his wife, and has bought her a gift he believes is for the soul, something that will truly mean something to her.

Karen, of course, doesn't see it this way. She wanted the expensive necklace. And she's well within her rights to have wanted the expensive necklace. Who spends £16.99 on their wife for Christmas? Harry the Boss is definitely Harry the Bastard. But Harry is not so much being a devious shit as being a complete sap. A man with as much grit as a pot of pasteurised yogurt.

Mia

Mia puts the necklace on, just in case you didn't know who he'd bought the necklace for, and pouts into the mirror like a total bitch.

Karen

A scene that has become folkloric in some circles, standing for every deceived and broken heart in the land. For some reason, insulted and heartbroken with the gift of a Joni Mitchell CD, Karen runs off to put it on, skipping straight to the end of it to play the title track. Thompson is excellent, not because she cries, battles the tears, battles the crushing disappointment of her life, but because during all this she straightens the bedclothes, a gesture to the fact, for the time being at least, her responsibilities to her family, to her domestic realm, and to her children's Christmas, and the memory of all Christmases to come, will not be destroyed by the pathetic idiocy of her husband, their father, Harry the Sap.

Daniel & Sam

Sam the Wise, the eleven-year-old with dead mummy issues, is giving therapy to his stepdad on the sofa. "How's your love life?" says the eleven-year-old to the widower of the mother he buried a week ago. Daniel replies with the usual appropriateness, making clear he is done with love, y'know, unless Claudia Schiffer[83] calls.

Poor old Claudia Schiffer, forever to be the go-to hottie for a generation of middle-class white men with no imagination (no offence to Claudia Schiffer).

This is also the scene where Daniel calls Sam "a wee motherless mongrel".

Bit harsh.

---

[83] If your eyes roll every time Richard Curtis uses supermodels to stand in for symbols of male desire, you'll end up needing an optometrist with a crowbar to set them right by the end of the film.

Christmas Eve

That's right, it's almost over.

Billy Mack

Billy Mack gets his Christmas Number One, which is cause for ironic celebration as he's still pretending he hates all this and he's actually a real rock 'n' roll star.[84] Elton John is immediately on the phone to invite Billy to a Christmas party for non-losers. It's a tough business. A business of Haves and Have Nots. Billy Mack is now a Have. And nobody is feeling that more right now than Rab C. Nesbitt, Billy Mack's manager, who not only is being called fat[85] and sad on national radio, but also is not getting the credit he deserves for being the genius behind this shameless cash grab and degradation of British music culture in the first place.

---

[84] A friend once commented to me that Billy Mack's distaste for his own single was akin to John Lydon's butter adverts of 2008. But as Lydon pointed out at the time, he was broke, and the money he took from the ads he put into a new tour for his finest band, Public Image Ltd. There's no suggestion in *Love Actually* that Billy Mack will be investing money from his resurrected cache into any musical projects that have any kind of integrity. That, you have to admit, might have been a nice way to round off Billy Mack's story arc.

[85] *Love Actually* fat-shaming moment #1,383

John & Judy

Clothed, and away from the set for the first time, Martin Freeman and Joanna Page have been on a date. They kiss, awkwardly, because they're both shy, and, hilariously, because they've both been not having sex on a film set for the last three weeks. This is irony. John, elated, jumps down the steps in such a strange, *small* way, it must have been the moment Peter Jackson thought Freeman would be perfect to play a hobbit jumping into lots of holes and caves and stuff.

Jamie

Uncle Jamie (much more palatable than "Uncle Billy") has turned up at a family do, arms weighed down with copious seasonal gifts, lots of nieces and nephews very happy to see him. But oh no, something has dropped, probably a penny, and he has to leave, abruptly. The kids now vocally hate Uncle Jamie, because you know what kids are like. It's Christmas Eve, but it doesn't matter, a man's got to do what a man's got to do, which in this case has nothing to do with the chivalrous code of the Old American West, but involves getting to St Pancras and then on to the Eurostar, which will take him directly to the family restaurant in France or Portugal or somewhere, where Aurelia is now waiting tables.

Sarah

We're moving at quite a pace now, as Curtis realises the movie has been going for ninety-five minutes and he needs to get his ducks in a row to wrap all this up. Sarah is in the office, where all sad unloved losers spend Christmas Eve. Not-so-Enigmatic Karl is there too, but that boat has sailed, I'm afraid, Sarah. The sex didn't happen, so any feelings that may have been felt are now null and void. It's regretful, but that's the way it goes. Them's the rules.

PM

More work from the ministerial red briefcase. Nobody is as lonely as lonely lonesome alone people at Christmas, no matter who you are.

Daniel & Sam

Daniel has made dinner. But Sam is practising the drums. Go away weird man, who just called me a motherless mongrel, I'm improving on the drums by pretending this snare is your face.

Sarah & Michael

She has gone to see her brother, who may or may not take a swing at her at any moment. Instead he hugs her. I guess that's the chances you have to take with mentally ill siblings. One day it's a broken jaw, the next day a warm embrace.

This also marks the end of Sarah's strand. It is so sad that she was forced, by the writer, to choose between love and her violently unwell institutionalised brother, that I almost can't quite handle it.

Mark & Juliet & Peter

The most ridiculed, parodied, and fucked-up scene in *Love Actually* in a hot contest for fucked-up scenes, is undoubtedly this one. It has passed into cultural folklore, parodied,[86] pilloried, praised; this is where Mark reveals his true feelings for Juliet through the medium of flash cards.[87] This is the first time Mark has attempted to talk to Juliet since he ran off to Dido in the streets. And it's quite clear Juliet has not told her husband that she's discovered his best mate has fallen hopelessly in love with/has a creepy video of her. Perhaps that could have been the moment when Peter huffs, rolls his eyes, and says to Juliet, "He always does this with my girlfriends. I thought he'd got over it. And maybe the fact I married you might have made him *grow up* a bit. Did I tell you he booked sex workers for

---

[86] Not least by Boris Johnson in one of an ongoing list of cringeworthy Johnson publicity stunts, this time as part of his successful 2019 General Election campaign.

[87] This is, of course, something of a parody in itself, taking the format most famously used by Bob Dylan (with a lurking Allen Ginsberg in the background) for his promo video for his 1965 song "Subterranean Homesick Blues". Two more different artistic statements you would struggle to find.

my stag do? Yes, I agree it's not even funny. No, nothing *happened*. It kind of ruined the night, if I'm honest with you. I asked them to leave. It got even worse. They were transsexuals. Well, of course that makes a difference. I don't know, it just *does*. No, I wouldn't have shagged them had they been *real* women. Biological women. Yes, I know transwomen are *real* women. So, I *should* have shagged them? Is that what you're saying? I should have shagged them because they were trans? So as not to cause offence? No, I didn't think so. Anyway, I'd already asked them to leave. It just makes a difference. No. How dare you. I'm not transphobic. It just wasn't that kind of party. They have just as much of a right to make a living as anybody else. Yeah, well maybe I made a mistake MARRYING *YOU*."

But this isn't the sliding door Richard Curtis went through. We all know much successful scripted comedy thrives on the contortions characters are willing to go to in order to maintain a lie. But this scene isn't really comedic. Here, Curtis has employed a golden tract of comedy – keeping the lie alive – in order to construct a purportedly *romantic*, not comedic interaction. Mark tells Juliet, via flashcard, to tell Peter it's carol singers at the door, and then puts on a CD that sounds like midnight mass at St Paul's Cathedral.[88] That Mark is supposed to be charming, cute, in this scene says a great deal. He's cute in the way a bunch of sexually aggressive white men drinking pints of vomit at a stag do is cute. He is selfish, spoiled, entitled, and Curtis gives him the strangest excuse for character motivation that seems to crop up again and again in *Love Actually*. The reason Mark is doing this is because Christmas is the time when people are supposed to tell the truth.

---

[88] Had Peter been at all interested, he may have wondered about the harp accompaniment. I, for one, would have been curious to come down the steps and take a look since this is not your average snotty bunch of kids in bobble hats.

Where Curtis has come up with this from, I'm not certain. It's certainly not something I've encountered as a tag line to any of my forty-plus Christmases on Earth. I can't find any evidence that people believe Christmas is a time when we must all tell the truth. In fact, all I have found is evidence for the opposite. Christmas should be a time where people should keep their opinions to themselves so as not to ruin Christmas.

Mark makes his way through his flash cards. Without ever being precise, we have been led to believe Mark has some kind of creative job. His flat is some kind of studio, he works in an art gallery. With this in mind, he might have spent a bit more time on his flash cards. They are scribbled. He gets to one that is a collage of magazine cuttings. Supermodels. Again. An entire flashcard of supermodels this time. This is really supposed to be funny, cute, charming. It's just a bit *gross*. Again, the laziest form of schoolyard onanistic aspiration. Let's not even get into the fact that "supermodels" in *Love Actually* are consistently used as functionary meat dolls, in this instance a way for Mark to claim he has a hope to obliterate all pangs of his inconvenient crush on his best mate's wife. Let's not get onto how insulting and fucked up it is for him to start a declaration of his undying love for Juliet (yes, he will love her until she is a cadaver, don't forget) with how he will hopefully be banging a supermodel this time next year, so don't worry about what I'm about to say. Juliet is won over. Of course she is; this is 2003 and she is eighteen and it looks as though her upbringing wasn't one mired in struggle, or one with easy access to the works of Gloria Steinem. Mark the Twat gets what he wants. No consequences. Job done, a man's gone done what a man had to go and get done, and he swaggers off down the mews like John Wayne in that last shot from *The Searchers* (1956); a smugger twat you will not see this Christmas.

But wait... something in Juliet has been awakened. She chases him, kisses him, with a look of hopeless sadness. Maybe she loves him too? Maybe she just feels sorry for him. It feels a bit more than that. A new affair? Something purer than Harry the Bastard's affair, less complexity, more entitlement, more of the animal energy of the youthful middle class. She goes back off to the cosy mews and to her cosy, clueless husband. Mark, smug as the proverbial fuck, turns to the camera and utters, as if exiting a scene from a sixth-form production of *As You Like It*, "Enough. Enough now." This is Curtis closing the curtain on this narrative strand. Nobody has been hurt. Love has been declared, and declared, as Mark's flashcard states, without expectation or even strategy. It is enough that it has been declared at all. It is enough and it is beautiful that we can all recognise the inconvenient, uncontrollable passions of the heart. And that is that. Nothing will change, apart from the air is purer with the rightful truth telling of love's glow. Juliet will go on loving her husband, and Mark will hopefully soon be having sex with Linda Evangelista, and Juliet will live her life between these two dreadful men, and all will be right with the world. Amen.

Billy Mack & Joe

Joe,[89] Billy Mack's long-suffering manager, is home watching the Billy Mack Christmas video surrounded by posters of Billy Mack in his Billy Mack room. Nothing weird there. Billy turns up with a bottle of rosé by the looks of things to tie up this strand. It's unclear whether this is a gay strand. If Curtis was tempted to turn it this way, he fluffs it. Mack is as obnoxious as always, and Nighy now is in full slurring, juddering, jackknife body language mode, his default acting style when he's lost at sea.[90] He declares some kind of love for Joe, although he still can't stop bullying him for his weight. It's unsure whether Joe is gay, but it's less unclear that he worships his charge, and that this campaign to get Mack back into the big time has been more than a calculated money-making venture. Joe *believes* in Billy; he believes in him as an artist and as a human. Joe is shocked at Billy's declaration of love. He offers to shake his hand, but Billy has a hug in mind. This isn't very gay. When Billy says, with one of the most repulsive glints in the history

---

[89] Rab C. Nesbitt

[90] Bill Nighy is mostly a joy to watch, and our preconceptions that he is a joy to watch does much of the heavy lifting in *Love Actually*.

of cinema, that he thinks they should get drunk and watch porn, Joe, who had planned on a Bailey's and milk and settling down for *It's a Wonderful Life* showing on BBC2 at 10pm, realises this is the life he has chosen, and that loving Billy Mack is not about love, but is about self-loathing. Self-loathing, after all, is all around.

PM

Prime Minister David realises he has been a fool, that he loves Natalie Doolittle and that nothing should get in the way of that. Especially not at Christmas. She has sent him a card, declaring herself his property, which is all he needed to hear. She knows the way to a man's genetically hard-wired sense of entitlement.[91] The PM has done a stupid thing, trying to insulate himself against his feelings by having Natalie cruelly shoved out of her job because of nothing she did wrong,[92] and now he wants to put it right by bulldozing her with his power and influence into becoming his concubine. He rallies the secret service, or whatever it is we have over here, drops his admin (which is of course

---

[91] Again, here we see this strange idea that Curtis has decided to hang the motivations of most of his characters on the fallacy there is a cultural relationship between Christmas and honesty. Curtis seems to be under the impression Christmas is known universally as the season of damn the consequences.

[92] Twice Natalie states that she is under the misapprehension she lost her job in Number 10 because Billy Bob Thornton's POTUS sexually harassed her, and that she was blamed. At no point does the PM correct her on this, and tell her that was not why she was moved from his office; rather it was because he wasn't sure he couldn't keep his hands off her himself.

what all PMs are doing on the evening of Christmas Eve), tells the Number 10 security guard not to wait up (because he's off to have sex with the tea lady/document deliverer), and then instructs his driver he wants to be taken to the rough end of Wandsworth because tonight, my good coachman, this evening my sexual predilections involve the degradations of the lower classes, and don't spare the horses. They have a police escort, sending them zipping over an empty Albert Bridge, sirens blaring as it helps the PM with his erection.

The PM doesn't know which house is Natalie's, so he has to go knocking on doors, rather than getting her address from HR. Here we have a nice collection of comedic set pieces that don't really feel to have reached their potential. Curtis's writing, throughout, exhibits a tiredness, a lack of energy and ideas, ironic for a film that is believed to contain so many iconic moments. That the PM is forced to sing a Christmas carol by three young girls and that his bodyguard, Gavin, turns out to have an operatic[93] singing voice, is a well-pitched scene. But Curtis seems to only be interested in presenting an *idea* of a comedic frame, without really seeing it through. The reason is most likely that *Love Actually* is too packed with story strands for any of the more successful moments to be allowed to breathe.[94]

---

[93] And Welsh.

[94] Some deleted story strands have passed into folklore. Some of these strands are available to see in the deleted scenes included as extra features of the *Love Actually* DVD. These include a story about ageing lesbian couple Anne Reid and Frances de la Tour, which seems to have been written for the soul purpose of having one of them tragically die of cancer (which, of course, is the fate of all lesbian couples in movies made by straight people); another has an African family joyously walking away from a failed crop looking forward with a gleeful light-heartedness to lives as refugees. It is for you decided whether it's to the credit of Curtis that these strands didn't make it into the final cut, or whether he should be brought up on the fact he shot them at all.

No sooner does this door-knocking sequence raise a smile, than a door is answered by Mia, Harry the Boss's secretary. She is Natalie's neighbour. There seems to be no reason for putting Mia in that house other than maybe they're trying to make her work for her money. The PM apologises for his crap Cabinet, and goes off to knock up Natalie, the gravity of his decision to come to her house unannounced beginning to dawn on him. This is not just a Downing Street blowjob now; there's a chance other people will know. What if Natalie's mum answers the door? What if it's her dad? What if it's her dad and he didn't vote for Grant? The horror. Oh dear. It's worse. It's the whole family. They are about to go out somewhere. The dog tracks or down the docklands to sell cockles and mussels or something. In fact, they are going to the school Christmas concert – remember that? – the climax of the film where everything will be tied together. The one that Sam is going to play drums to win the heart of the girl with the same name as his dead mother. Natalie's mother explains this school Christmas concert will be the first time ever this many schools have come together, which is useful, because for a second there we were supposed to believe Emma Thompson's kids were at the same school as kids from the rough end of Wandsworth. Which makes it all the more strange, then, that Curtis is aware enough of working-class experience to know that the working-class children of London have a very different educational experience to the middle- and upper-middle class kids of London, and yet is still so tone-deaf to the working-class voice. Natalie, because she's a rough diamond, comes down the stairs swearing like a sailor: "Any of you fuckers seen my fucking coat, you bunch of fucking fuckers?" she asks her family including about five children. Because this is funny, and it's how working-class people communicate with one another. Looks like her time working with Prime Minister 'enry 'iggins has done nothing for her couthness. Perhaps it's hardly surprising, though, that she swears in front of children and elderly relatives like a pirate with Tourette syndrome when she has had to go through her life being fat-shamed even by her own father; he here refers to her by the long-standing family nickname, "Plumpy". It's difficult to truly understand how anybody, even in the dark ages of 2003, could think this was a legitimate, and funny, running joke. The joke is presumably that Martine McCutcheon is definitely not "carrying any weight" (as my mum would have put it). The joke doesn't work though because, even if you remove the bullying at its base, it is explored and delivered with timid laziness. The PM, the only person bemused by the recurrence of references to Natalie's weight, is not bemused enough to follow through, to investigate or interrogate. Is the PM experiencing a *Shallow Hal* (2001)[95] moment? And are we? Of course, to an extent none of that matters, because the running joke is cruel and offensive. But also, it speaks of the wider disengagement Curtis displays with his once-immaculate understanding of the mechanics of jokes. This scene does however contain perhaps the funniest line of the whole film, when Natalie's mother explains the importance of the school concert: "The octopus costume has taken me months. Eight is a lot of legs, David."[96] The PM offers to

---

[95] *Shallow Hal*, a misfiring comedy from the notorious Farrelly brothers, has one over on *Love Actually*, in that while Jack Black's Hal is put under a spell where he sees fat-suited Gwyneth Paltrow in her real slender form, he grows as a person. There is no evidence of anybody growing in *Love Actually*.

[96] Although it may be a bit of a stretch to suggest that *Love Actually* could have been a better film, even a great film, had there been as much inspiration elsewhere as you find this line, it is a joke that takes the memory to many of the great lines from *Blackadder*. However, it should also be noted that when Curtis was the sole scriptwriter for that series, i.e. its entire first season, *Blackadder* was dreadful. It was only with the addition of Ben Elton to form a writing partnership with Curtis from season two that the

give Natalie a lift to the concert, and the rest of the family all pile into the back of the police escort car, an environment probably more than familiar to all of them as they're all working class and no doubt have all been arrested at some point due to their working-class criminal endeavours or something.

The PM wants to tell Natalie he loves her, and she is still apologetic for being sexually harassed by Billy Bob Thornton. The PM sticks to the position of not correcting her on the assumption she was sacked because of this encounter with POTUS and thus relieving her from what is clearly a substantial emotional trauma. Between them, in a well-judged comedic juxtaposition, is Natalie's toddler brother in octopus costume. Natalie, against all the odds, manages to not swear during this entire exchange, suggesting she is already lifting herself out of the slums of working-class vocabulary.[97] She tells the PM that she loves him. Come to the concert, she says. The PM, in an alarming moment of self-awareness, judges that nobody wants a sleazy politician turning up at a children's concert. Hope you didn't want kids, Natalie.

---

programme reached its position as towering achievement of British comedy. Coincidence?

[97] Although Curtis has made much hay out of getting posh people to say "fuck", such as in the famous opening of *Four Weddings and a Funeral* in which Hugh Grant repeats the word ad infinitum as he runs late to the first of the four weddings. It must be something to do with accents.

Judy & John

For some reason Judy and John are at the concert, and some random bloke[98] asks how they met. They look embarrassed, awkward, because they can only think of the answer, "We met simulating a wide array of sexual positions including consensual scatological games, as body doubles in a big-budget movie" rather than, "We met at work".

If you didn't know it a long time ago, it is now blindingly apparent we all could have saved ourselves a lot of time had Curtis left this entire strand on the cutting room floor.

---

[98] John's brother, apparently.

Daniel & Sam

In the car park, Daniel tries to stick down Sam's hair with spit fingers because now he's his mother, and Sam swipes at him with his drumsticks like a right little shit.

Jamie

And just like that, as if he had his own private jet, Jamie is in Marseille.

PM & Natalie

Natalie leans into the open window of the PM's car and says she's managed to sort it out and they can watch the concert from the wings backstage. The PM doesn't look overjoyed at this idea. He wanted his Christmas Downing Street blowjob. Bill Clinton definitely didn't have to go and watch Monica Lewinsky's nephews sing "Silent Night" to get his oats. But our PM agrees, because surely, after that, he's in like Flynn.

PM & Natalie & Karen

Remember that Karen is the PM's sister, and as he and Natalie and his bodyguard (he of the Male Voice Choir extraction) dart through the shadowy corridors of the backstage school area, brother and sister collide. Karen holds him hard, welling up, the emotions of the day, of the revelation of her devious cheating sad sack of a husband, all come to the surface. What she needs is a pillar, her brother. It's a shame in some ways that his advice to her isn't to stop being a sissy as no one is going to shag her if she's crying all the time. But even a PM who goes off on a strange tangent about his paedo uncle while he's being introduced to his house staff knows better than to talk that way to someone going through a life trauma. It's sad, however, that Karen, in a bit of a bad way emotionally, thinks David has turned up for her, after much nagging of his secretary, and he allows her to believe that too, just like he allows Natalie to believe she was sacked for being sexually harassed by POTUS. He's not overly keen on owning up to things, this guy.[99] The PM is then forced to introduce

---

[99] Certainly a trait of modern politics, and most brazenly epitomised in the characters of both Tony Blair and Boris Johnson.

Natalie, who he rather charmingly refers to as his "catering manager". "Careful he keeps his hands off you," says Karen, somewhat indiscreetly. "Twenty years ago, you'd have been just his type." A bit of rough.

The Concert

Almost there.

Still no explanation, even in the terms of an absurdist joke, why there are so many sea creatures at the nativity, but I guess we can put that down to a missed opportunity for an enlivening comedic sequence from the imagination of Curtis.

The concert itself is a mercifully brief affair. Little Joanna (not Dead-Mum Joanna) sings "All I Want for Christmas", arguably on the "sexier" side of Christmas hits for an eleven-year-old, but still, actress Olivia Olson does all her own vocal work, channelling the warbled prosthetics of Christina Aguilera. And there is Sam on the drums, thinking he's got this nailed, blissfully unaware of just how much therapy he requires, the need for which increases with intensity every passing day that his stepfather neglects to get him some. Joanna reaches the climax and when Sam realises that she doesn't just mean all she wants for Christmas is *him*, but also someone else and someone else and someone else, and that maybe it's a just a song and she's performing it, a look descends across his face that must worry every woman who has the potential to cross paths with this burgeoning psycho for years to come. It is a chilling moment. And not very cute.

The song ends, and a centre-stage scenery board pulls back to reveal a Merry Christmas banner, but instead reveals the PM and his catering manager having a good old snog. Whoops. His poll ratings are likely now to go through the roof.

Karen & Harry

The detritus of a successful multi-school, mixed-posh-and-poor-kids Christmas concert. The goodbyes and the season's well wishes. But such moments can bring astounding clarity. Karen confronts Harry. "What would you do," she asks, "if you found out your husband had bought a solid gold necklace and given it to someone else?" Harry is revealed for the sap that he is. His shoulders drop, as if he has just been given the invoice for the M.O.T. on his car. Curtis, unable to arouse the most basic of contrition speeches in his man, sinks back to a strange cod-Shakespearean form of expression, something that makes Mark's "Enough. Enough now" seem less of an accident. "I am *so* in the wrong," says Harry, which is hard to argue with. "A classic fool," he says, as if this superficial contrition offered up in archaic phraseology wraps everything up neatly. Is this three-word line a wink and maybe even a nod to what Curtis thinks *Love Actually* is in his head: a modern Shakespearean comedy, *As You Like Much Ado About a Shrew*?[100]

---

[100] Another interesting revelation on the DVD commentary is that this scene wasn't originally in the script, but Rickman asked for it, as he felt that this arc needed completing. Odd that the script writer hadn't originally thought of that himself.

Daniel & Sam

Liam Neeson bursts through school corridor swing doors with that physical presence that was to make him a global action movie icon in his sixties, only this time he has a big wide grin on his face. *Sam did it!* He won the heart of his prize, and all the world will be right because he definitely doesn't need therapy, not one single hour of the stuff thank you very much.

But what's this? Sam is sad, almost defeated. Joanna (not his dead mum) doesn't love him after all. The drumming plan didn't work. What is wrong with the world? Daniel won't let this slide, though. He'll be buggered if he's going to have to fork out for the kid's therapy. Seen all those movies? Where the guy chases the woman in the airport? Those big romantic gestures. This is what's called for. Because Joanna (not his dead mum) is flying back to the States tonight. On Christmas Eve.

Sam lights up. It may not work, but it'll be a bit of fun. And then, high-fiving his dad (yes, he calls him Dad for the first time – big moment), Sam delivers perhaps the worst line of the film, and possibly in movie history. It is a line that I find myself having a physical reaction to, as if it tickles the bacteria in my stomach. But I also have a moral reaction to it, as if it's a crime against humanity, and as if by making a small boy say it should constitute jail time for Richard Curtis. Sam says...

> "Let's do it. Let's go and get the shit kicked out of us by love."

I am convinced by this point that Curtis believes his movie is an updated Shakespearean comedy about love, and this is the type of line he thinks the Bard would be writing if he were alive today. It's the type of thinking that has found its way into some quarters in the last few decades, as people who believe "guilty pleasures" are things that need justifying, things that need qualifying and heightening. So, you have the argument that if Dickens were alive today, he would be writing for *Eastenders*. Or if the Beatles formed now, they would be Take That. I think that anybody who finds warmth in the line "Let's go and have the shit kicked out of us by love" probably deserve to have the shit kicked out of them by hobnail boots.

Daniel & Carol

Every now and again in *Love Actually*, there is a flash of something deeper. But only a flash. A flash subdued by the torrents of misjudged, misguided, badly written, offensive, humourless toilet water that swells around it. This short scene embodies this perfectly.

Daniel collides with another parent. This parent is played by Claudia Schiffer,[101] which reminds us that *Love Actually* was written by a teenage boy who worships supermodels as ideals of female sexuality. Curtis here will leave us without a doubt that Daniel will get together with the Schiffer lookalike (actually Schiffer) in the future, beyond the boundaries of this film's time frame. But when Schiffer-not-Schiffer introduces herself as Carol, Daniel calls her "Karen", for which Schiffer-not-Schiffer needs to correct him. Realising his mistake, Daniel rolls his eyes, bites his lip. He has to be careful of that. Saying Karen's name. Because he cannot allow it to become apparent that he

---

[101] Schiffer was reportedly paid in the region of £200,000 for her one-minute appearance, suggesting that Curtis' repeated references to supermodels were because he believed that they were essential to the comedic backbone of *Love Actually* and not just lazy writing. Which is worse is down to you to decide.

is actually in love with Karen. Always has been. Harry's downtrodden Joni Mitchell-educated Karen. The one who finds it difficult to really engage with Daniel. That one. A tragic story of star-crossed lovers.

Outside, Daniel and Sam see Not-Dead-Mum Joanna getting very very very very slowly into a car. Have they missed their chance? Worry not! Daniel knows a shortcut to the airport. Even though a shortcut doesn't seem necessary, as Joanna has literally just pulled away.

Jamie

Strong joke here of mistaken identity, when Jamie, newly arrived in Marseille, a place I only really know for their football team of the eighties and nineties that Chris Waddle played for, and as the place of Popeye Doyle's excruciating heroin cold turkey in *French Connection II* (1975), asks Aurelia's father for her hand in marriage. Only, Dad thinks he's there for his other daughter, who is ugly and unmarriable and (of course) fat. It's a tired, lazy joke, more light and forgettable than it is offensive, but it is still offensive and yet another joke for which the basis is a woman's appearance. And it's forgotten by all involved no sooner than it's set up and played out. Dad says he will take Jamie to Aurelia, mix-up brushed aside, and he leads him out into the cobbled street. They begin to gather followers like Rocky Balboa scaling the steps outside the Philadelphia Museum of Art. This will be a feat of comparable strength and determination should Jamie pull it off.

Daniel & Sam

A good ol' airport finale it is then, for the twisted duo of Daniel and Sam. It'll go right to the wire – or departure gate – you mark my words.

Jamie

We're staying with the fat jokes for Aurelia's sister. Her dad calls her "Miss Dunkin' Donuts 2003", and now we're under the suspicion that Curtis is just using jokes that get said around the house by his kids.

Daniel & Sam

It's gone right to the departure gate. There's a stick-in-the-mud jobsworth who won't let Daniel and Sam any further without a boarding pass. "Not even to let the boy say goodbye to the love of his life?" says Daniel, trying not to sound threatening, but it's not easy when you're Liam Neeson. It's to the airline official's credit that he remains steadfast on this, seeing as 9/11 was just a year or so ago, and actually formed the central theme of the prologue speech of this very movie. Daniel, showing the judgement we have come to expect from this towering symbol of fatherhood, encourages Sam to make a run for it, shielded from the authorities by the knowing fussiness of a second Rowan Atkinson[102] cameo. Sam slips through, taking with him the risk of being gunned down by airport security as a suspected al-Qaida human child bomb. The things we do for love.

---

[102] Rowan Atkinson's Rufus makes a second, random appearance here to provide a decoy, a cameo that is less jarring if you know he is an angel, which we don't, because the moment where Rufus walks off and then disappears in a puff of smoke was cut. Which is a damn shame. It also raises the question what other stupid moment could have been heightened with a touch of ethereal Atkinson magic?

So, Sam runs, the music swells, the Keystone Airport Security Guards[103] are no match for the power of love, and he gets to the departure gate, sees Joanna, cries out her name, but she can't hear him. My god, will love not prevail?

---

[103] A golden rule of reviewing is that you must comment on what is there, and not what you, the critic, wish to see there, but it's very hard not to think how a well-choregraphed Keystone Cops chaotic cavalcade of chase here would have heightened this stretch of the movie.

Jamie

Jamie and his band of supporters march on through the cobbled streets of Marseille. Chinese whispers have been feeding through the throng, and halfway back a woman seems to think they are following Jamie to watch him murder Aurelia. Curtis, yet again, shows he will not allow an opportunity to pass without capturing it with a wildly inappropriate and unfunny joke.

Sam & Not-Dead-Mum Joanna

The Keystone Guards have given up chasing Sam through the airport. Let the human child bomb explode, they say, bent over trying to catch their breaths. Let the chips fall where they may. Sam reaches another security barrier, but Billy Mack is on a television screen, performing naked as he promised he would if he hit the Christmas Number One spot, and this inspires Sam to jump the barrier. What a pantheon of heroes this boy has.

Joanna doesn't seem weirded out by Sam's presence, which is good, because she probably has a whole lifetime ahead of her of males pestering her when she's just trying to go about her daily life. But *Love Actually* is a man's film, if nothing else, and the girl is not embarrassed, not angry, that the little drummer boy pulled this bit of theatre in front of her parents. Indeed, when Sam is strong-armed by the Keystone Guards, who had a change of heart and eventually catch up with him, Joanna follows him back in order to give him a peck on the cheek. Not annoying, but charming. Winning.

Jamie & Aurelia

Jamie and the throng reach the restaurant where Aurelia waits tables, so that Jamie, using the Facebook translator by the looks of things, can ask her to marry him. It's romantic, because there is nothing a woman likes more than to have a man come in and embarrass her in her place of work. As an opening gesture of their new engagement, showing Aurelia that he has no respect for her professional space is maybe not Jamie's strongest move, but this is not a Nora Ephron movie, so Aurelia, and the rest of Marseille, find this a glowing romantic gesture and cheer at the union. Sprinkle in a few more fat jokes and even a skinny slur – is no woman the right size and shape for Richard Curtis? – and we have that strand, and Christmas, all sewn up. *Graças a deus por isso.*

1 Month Later (Epilogue)

The denouement, bypassing what might have been an interesting Christmas Day. Curtis takes us straight to late January and a compendium of loose ends being tied up in the arrival lounge of Heathrow,[104] This all happens to the tune of the Beach Boys' "God Only Knows";[105] not a Christmas song, but anyway, it's now late January so I guess that doesn't matter so much.

Billy Mack returns from some trip involving international stardom. Joe, not the homosexual love of Billy's life as it turns out, gets the name wrong of the supermodel-esque woman Billy has brought with him, cementing his journey from washed-up joke to womanising Rockstar. "This one's Greta," he slithers, making the woman hardly discernible from his luggage.

---

[104] Actually, a set, the cost of which sucked more than half of the *Love Actually* budget, so I'm told. The rest going to Claudia Schiffer. No wonder the British film industry is a bust-and-boom economy.

[105] There's an odd religious theme running through this film, what with Atkinson being an angel and all. I don't know if Curtis is a believer, but he seems willing to suggest some kind of higher power at work. As with the film's politics, he's happy to both eat and retain his cake.

If you remember that far back, Jamie was at Juliet and Peter's wedding, and so they come here to welcome him and Aurelia to England, with Mark who admits he's "just tagging along", which I guess is something Peter's going to have to get used to now his wife is engaged in a cruelly ambiguous emotional tryst with her husband's best man. If music be the food of free love, fill yer boots.

Harry the Boss is back, lifting his little daughter with such a huff you'd be forgiven for thinking Curtis has a fat joke in the barrel of his gun. Karen is there too, but things are tepid, this is the beginning of the long road back to a happy marriage where Harry can pretend he doesn't recognise Joni Mitchell's voice. Oh, but hang on, it's probably not a good idea to mention Joni Mitchell anymore. Not after the Christmas present fiasco.

Sam is meeting Not-Dead-Mum Joanna off the plane. Daniel is there with Not Claudia Schiffer, so that worked out well, although he must be running out of excuses as to why he keeps calling her Karen during sex.

Judy and John make a quick appearance, because Curtis is under the impression anyone cares about what happened to them. Well, they got married. So, they're in this scene because they just came back from their honeymoon, unless they just got married in the airport chapel? John says a strange thing as Judy gleefully flashes her wedding ring. "Might get a shag now." This is supposed to be an ironic joke, because the two of them met simulating sex acts. But it just makes Judy seem prudish, or perhaps she holds a deeply conservative religious belief that belies the depth of her character and, indeed, her profession.

They lurch onto Tony, the director of their movie, and also friend of sex tourist psycho-in-the-making Colin. Yes, we have to finish this movie with Colin, a strong contender with Billy Mack for most repulsive single character in this whole sorry mess. Colin returns with a girl, bringing his sexual psychosis out of the fantasia of his damaged mind into the reality of the *Love Actually* world. He has also brought with him a "gift" for Tony, in the form of Denise Richards's sexually aggressive idea of what an uber-desirable American "hottie" looks and acts like. The best way to read this, the only way to keep your dinner down, is that all this is split between two perspectives: the fantasy of Colin, and that of Tony who now realises, seeing Colin is introducing him to two women who are not actually there, that his friend is schizophrenically delusional. When we see Denise Richards kiss Tony, we are seeing the world through Colin's eyes. When we see Tony's surprised face, we are seeing the world through Tony's eyes. Because nobody is there. Colin, with the crazed eyes of a killer, is introducing Tony to thin air.

And the final fictional moment goes to the PM, and in particular his bodyguards who don't bat an eyelid when a blur of red pushes out of the crowd and dives onto the body of their charge. Luckily, it's Natalie, and not an assassin, raining down kisses and not knives and bombs.

And that, as they say, is that.

Although it isn't...

Love Actually now slips seamlessly from the fictional world of airport arrivals to the real world of airport arrivals, with a montage of families reunited after trips. It has echoes of the opening, bookending the movie, even if the reason is a little muddied. This is love. Love in all its forms. Dirty, messy, complicated, beautiful and human. The screen splits, and splits again, like *Rashomon* (1950), like a mediocre Brian De Palma movie, only this is not about revenge or violence or murder; this is about love, in all its forms, family connections, longing, lust, friendship, dependability, responsibility, disappointment, selfishness, self-love, masturbation, fat jokes, misogyny, sexual harassment, stalking, adultery, transphobia, homophobia, Uncle Billy, paedophilia, Joni Mitchell, simulated sex, and love. Yes, it's all about love.

Afterword

So, where does that leave us? Few things make me more frustrated than going on a journey and ending up in exactly the same place where I started (I'm looking at you, season three of *Games of Thrones*); but I'm afraid the faint hope I held in my heart at the outset of this dubious project, the one that made me think I may grow to respect, maybe admire, and yes, possibly even love, *Love Actually*, came to nothing. I did not come to love it. Or even like it. In fact, when the dust settled, the tears dried from my eyes, and the spittle was wiped from the corner of the mouth, it became apparent that I had grown to despise it even more. Before embarking on this book, it seems, I only really had a general dislike for a film that was defined to me by some glaring moments of ugliness and poor taste. What I discovered with this semi-forensic exploration of the film is that it is actually much worse than I ever remembered or even might have imagined. Okay, so I discovered I quite like Colin Firth's performance, but as I explained, I am an admirer of Firth (particularly for his performance in Tom Ford's *A Single Man*), so I'm not learning anything new there. And I came to realise that perhaps there is a little more nuance to the Harry–Karen story than many people give it credit for. Harry is crying out for help and is not just a "classic fool". Fine. Bravo. But that's all small change from two hours and eight minutes. What I really found out is that the film is an unrelenting cavalcade of mean-spirited, poorly crafted dross. It is not, by any reasonable definition, a warm-hearted Christmas classic. It has a cold heart, it doesn't understand anything about Christmas, and it falls well short of being a classic kind of anything. It's like an anxiety dream, each scene unfolding into view with a selection box of horrors. If you have any respect for the ability of human people to respect one another, then this film must leave you dejected. If you respect any living thing other than just white men, then this film must be a depressing watch for you. If you have any love for the craft and art of cinema, then this film must leave you weeping in the foetal position. If you have ever experienced love, and have cherished that feeling, then this film must leave you confused. *Love Actually* is less a film and more like a programme of extreme rendition. At its heart is not love, but rather a concrete room in a remote desert of an affiliate country, with one chair at its centre and single naked light bulb swinging menacingly from the ceiling. A CIA agent from behind plexiglass says in a sinister, quiet tone, "Imagine, if you will, spending Christmas with these people." *I give up*, you scream; *I want out. Ask me anything. I'm all yours.*

But this must have been worth something. I must have learned things that are worthwhile. Well, I have learned that Richard Curtis is a bad writer, but an even worse director. As a writer, he has a very poor feel for the killer line, the zinger. Obviously, the line that sticks out in *Love Actually* is "Let's go and have the shit kicked out of us by love", but the film is full of duds. But it doesn't seem to matter. People forgive Curtis for all the bad lines he can come up with. Nobody is in any doubt that the line "Is it raining? I hadn't noticed" is perhaps bad enough to have Curtis dragged up in front of a Hague war crime tribunal, and yet it does nothing to dampen the regard in which *Four Weddings and a Funeral*, the climax of which this line plays a significant part, is held. (It's impressive just what an elegiac bit of Auden can do to fog up the memories of an offended audience.) But it's worth noting just how often Curtis decries his own writing. In the DVD commentary (which is an artful exercise in cringe, featuring Curtis, a largely embarrassed Nighy, an extremely oily Hugh Grant, and the bemused child figurine of Thomas Brodie-Sangster), Curtis can be frequently heard referring to his dialogue in much the same way Billy Mack refers to his Christmas Number One. Curtis doesn't seem to have much respect for the art of screenwriting, and even if his attitude is false modesty (he has much to be modest about, to quote Winston Churchill) he seems painfully aware of his shortcomings as a writer of dialogue. You have to wonder, then, what he thinks of his own success, given he is, ostensibly, a screenwriter. Is this all just a joke to him, and a prank on us? The commentary on the DVD also offers up some other gentle nudges, ones that help us understand more the overt misogyny of the released film, and much of the entitled arrogance that underlies it. A great deal of the commentary is given over to Curtis and Grant leching over female cast members, particularly Keira Knightley, Sienna Guillory, Martine McCutcheon, Joanna Page, Heike Makatsch, Denise Richards, January Jones, Ivana Milićević, Claudia Schiffer, Elisha Cuthbert... well, yes, all of them apart from Emma Thompson, really. In the commentary, Nighy sounds a little reluctant, shy even, and enters into the Curtis–Grant bants only after a while, and even then, it's half-hearted. The DVD special features are interesting, in fact, and I haven't gone into too much detail on them here because they only really serve to further illustrate the things for which the film should be damned. They do not enlighten, they only entrench. In the deleted scenes there are more fat jokes (mainly directed at Emma Thompson's arse, which is the size of a shipping yard, apparently), and more aggressive sexual harassment from Nighy's Billy Mack ("Have you ever given a really old man a blowjob?" he asks a female record company employee who he at first mocked for looking twelve years old).

There is, I have had to conclude, nothing in the transtextual universe of *Love Actually* to redeem either the film or its writer and director. Since its release, Curtis has gone on to make more successful bad films. He has directed just two, *The Boat That Rocked* (2009) and *About Time* (2013); two truly terrible films riddled with much of the same elements that make *Love Actually* so objectionable. He has written more. Spielberg's strangely dull adaptation of stage sensation *War Horse* (2011) is perhaps the biggest surprise in Curtis's oeuvre because it brings him outside of his middle-class English romcom (dis)comfort zone. The sequel to *Mamma Mia!* (for which he wrote the story, and not the script) and a film about a world without Beatles songs are perhaps less surprising. But they are all bad (especially *Yesterday*, the one about the Beatles songs, which made me wish for a world without Beatles songs so that the idea for this movie could never have been hatched in the first place).

Another thing I have learned is that *Love Actually* could never be a guilty pleasure for me, in the way that *Bridget Jones* might be (oh-so dated, but it has some things going for it), or even *Mamma Mia!* (full of winning, full-throttle performances, and a decent script that Curtis didn't write). Never at any point during the writing of this book have I enjoyed watching a second of the film. All the hours I've spent sitting in front of it, and every second has been absolute shit for me. That's right. Absolute shit. But that doesn't mean there hasn't been some value in what has ultimately seen a reinforcement of my understanding that *Love Actually* is not just a bad movie but is a movie that is bad for you. It is a time capsule, yes, back to the liberally complacent 2003, when after 9/11 the enemy was conveniently without, not within, when millions of people didn't think twice about laughing at lazy fat jokes and casual misogyny. We are better at this stuff now, isn't that right? But that doesn't explain why *Love Actually* continues to be watched by so many and regarded with such devotion. Why does it have a hold on otherwise engaged people who I know to have admirable analytic faculties at their disposal? And why... why oh, why... were we treated to a sequel?

That's right, in 2017, Richard Curtis got much of the band back together for an update for his Comic Relief annual charity fundraiser. The sequel, *Red Nose Day Actually*, if you haven't seen it, is a rehash of all the "greatest" moments of the original, boiled down to their natural essence in a fifteen-minute sketch version.[106] Thirteen years later, thirteen years of progress, of social awakenings, of corrective thinking on matters of inappropriateness, gendered bigotry, and liberalism, and Richard Curtis comes back with a rehash of many of the most problematic moments. So, we see flashcards (of course – what is *Love Actually* without the flashcards?), we see the puerile fetishisation of supermodels, the fat jokes, and Billy Mack parading his sexual predatoriness.[107] The tag line is *Where Are They Now?* and it seems as though they are exactly where they were in 2003. So, they have progressed in terms of careers, relationships, and age, (a superficial progress, you might say), but there is no danger of them having evolved,

---

[106] the American version is seventeen minutes as it includes a revisit to Laura Linney's character that the UK version did not.
[107] This time he can't remember which one of the Kardashians he has had sex with.

either emotionally, politically, or sensitively. The characters have been in stasis. The fact is, it's the creators of *Love Actually* who have gotten nowhere in thirteen years. And, you could assume, it is the fans of the film who have encouraged this lack of reflection. So, I hope this book creates a corner of reflection where perhaps there wasn't one before; a room of contemplation that can be saved for those who watch *Love Actually* in this new age of liberal sensitivity and know you are not alone, and you are not even a minority. And when all the reflecting is done, I hope maybe it can be a space where we can perhaps collectively scream into the void. All readers and watchers together. Now, the silent scream, that's something that we can all relate to at Christmas, isn't it?

So... Merry Christmas one and all.

Acknowledgements

Thanks to Richard Davies at Parthian for saying yes to this; to David Cottis for going all in on the edit and effortlessly entering into the spirit; to Lisa Smithstead for a better foreword than I had any right to hope for; for everyone at Parthian working so hard on such a fast turnaround; to Carolyn Hitt, Hannah Hammad, Siân Owen, (and others) for their engagement and encouragement on the subject; to the countless souls now lost to the mists of time who have helped me deconstruct this film in various pubs and kitchens at parties over the years; always to Amelia for keeping me honest and telling me when my jokes aren't funny; and to Howie, my cat, who sat with me over a series of lockdown dawns while I watched *Love Actually* over and over – my sentinel and critical daemon.

About the authors

Gary Raymond is a novelist, critic, editor, and broadcaster. He is presenter of *The Review Show* for BBC Radio Wales and editor of *Wales Arts Review*. He is a regular writer on film, music, literature, and theatre, and can often be heard on BBC Radio 3 and 4 as an arts commentator and reviewer. His novels include *For Those Who Come After* (Parthian, 2015), *The Golden Orphans* (Parthian, 2018), and *Angels of Cairo* (Parthian, 2021).

Dr Lisa Smithstead is a senior lecturer in film studies. She is the author of various books and articles on film and literary history, including *The Boundaries of the Literary Archive: Reclamation and Representation* (with Carrie Smith, Routledge, 2013), *Off to the Pictures: Women's Writing, Cinemagoing and Movie Culture in Interwar Britain* (Edinburgh University Press, 2016), and *Reframing Vivien Leigh: Stardom, Gender and the Archive* (Oxford University Press, 2021).

Also by Gary Raymond

Angels of Cairo
Out June 2021
ISBN 978-1-913640-28-6 • £8.99

Just how far would you go to sacrifice for your art?

Told over a single day, Gary Raymond's latest novel is a fast-paced, sharp-edged comedy capturing a lifetime of angst and self-doubt, reminiscent of the writing of Graham Greene and Evelyn Waugh.

The Golden Orphans
Out now
ISBN 978-1-912109-13-5 • £8.99

A *Bookseller* Pick of the Week
'A sharp, pacy novel that has all the best hallmarks of the literary thriller' **Patrick McGuiness**

A dark, fast-paced literary thriller in the tradition of Graham Greene and Patricia Highsmith, but with a fresh, contemporary touch that is all its own.

PARTHIAN

PARTHIAN

MODERN WALES

WALES: ENGLAND'S COLONY?

Martin Johnes

From the very beginnings of Wales, its people have defined themselves against their large neighbour. This book tells the fascinating story of an uneasy and unequal relationship between two nations living side-by-side.

PB / £8.99
978-1-912681-41-9

RHYS DAVIES: A WRITER'S LIFE

Meic Stephens

Rhys Davies (1901-78) was among the most dedicated, prolific and accomplished of Welsh prose writers. This is his first full biography.

'This is a delightful book, which is itself a social history in its own right, and funny.'
– The Spectator

PB / £11.99
978-1-912109-96-8

MERTHYR, THE CRUCIBLE OF MODERN WALES

Joe England

Merthyr Tydfil was the town where the future of a country was forged: a thriving, struggling surge of people, industry, democracy and ideas. This book assesses an epic history of Merthyr from 1760 to 1912 through the focus of a fresh and thoroughly convincing perspective.

PB / £18.99
978-1-913640-05-7

TO HEAR THE SKYLARK'S SONG

Huw Lewis

To Hear the Skylark's Song is a memoir about how Aberfan survived and eventually thrived after the terrible disaster of the 21st of October 1966.

'A thoughtful and passionate memoir, moving and respectful.'
– Tessa Hadley

PB / £8.99
978-1-912109-72-2

ROCKING THE BOAT

Angela V. John

This insightful and revealing collection of essays focuses on seven Welsh women who, in a range of imaginative ways, resisted the status quo in Wales, England and beyond during the nineteenth and twentieth centuries.

PB / £11.99
978-1-912681-44-0

TURNING THE TIDE

Angela V. John

This rich biography tells the remarkable tale of Margaret Haig Thomas (1883-1958) who became the second Viscountess Rhondda. She was a Welsh suffragette, held important posts during the First World War and survived the sinking of the *Lusitania*.

PB / £17.99
978-1-909844-72-8

BRENDA CHAMBERLAIN, ARTIST & WRITER

Jill Piercy

The first full-length biography of Brenda Chamberlain chronicles the life of an artist and writer whose work was strongly affected by the places she lived, most famously Bardsey Island and the Greek island of Hydra.

PB / £11.99
978-1-912681-06-8